Pursuing God, Chasing Your Dreams, and Never EVER Giving Up On Yourself

Ricky Borba

TRILOGY CHRISTIAN PUBLISHERS
Tustin, CA

Trilogy Christian Publishers
A Wholly Owned Subsidiary of Trinity Broadcasting Network
2442 Michelle Drive
Tustin, CA 92780

Pursuing God, Chasing Your Dreams, and Never EVER Giving Up On Yourself

Copyright © 2023 by Ricky Borba

Stick Man art by Gabi Giles

Scripture quotations marked CEV are taken from the Contemporary English Version®. Copyright © 1995 American Bible Society. All rights reserved.

Scripture quotations marked ESV are taken from the ESV® Bible (The Holy Bible, English Standard Version®), copyright © 2001 by Crossway Bibles, a publishing ministry of Good News Publishers. Used by permission. All rights reserved.

Scripture quotations marked NIV are taken from THE HOLY BIBLE, NEW INTERNATIONAL VERSION®, NIV® Copyright © 1973, 1978, 1984, 2011 by Biblica, Inc.® Used by permission. All rights reserved worldwide.

All rights reserved, including the right to reproduce this book or portions thereof in any form whatsoever.

For information, address Trilogy Christian Publishing

Rights Department, 2442 Michelle Drive, Tustin, CA 92780.

Trilogy Christian Publishing/TBN and colophon are trademarks of Trinity Broadcasting Network.

For information about special discounts for bulk purchases, please contact Trilogy Christian Publishing.

Trilogy Disclaimer: The views and content expressed in this book are those of the author and may not necessarily reflect the views and doctrine of Trilogy Christian Publishing or the Trinity Broadcasting Network.

10 9 8 7 6 5 4 3 2 1

Library of Congress Cataloging-in-Publication Data is available.

ISBN 979-8-89041-351-2

ISBN (ebook) 979-8-89041-352-9 (ebook)

For my mom. Thank you for always believing in me.

Contents

Endorsement vii

Prologue Before the Prologue x

Prologue xiv

Chapter 1: God is in the Business of Showing Off and He Wants to Show Off Through YOU 1

Chapter 2: Identity 14

Chapter 3: Pressing into God, AKA: Trust 29

Chapter 4: How Are You Defining Success? 37

Chapter 5: How to Properly Deal with the Hardships/Rejection That Come With Following Your Dreams 47

Chapter 6: Myth-Breaking 61

Chapter 7: The World Needs You to Follow Your Dreams Because YOU Are the Only One Who Can Do It Your Way! 70

Chapter 8: Your Dreams and Visions From God Are What *May* Come True. Not of What *Will* Come True 75

Chapter 9: In Addition to Following Your Own Dreams and NEVER Giving Up, You're Also Called to Support Other People's Dreams 82

Chapter 10: Stay Humble in Your Success 87

Chapter 11: My Inspirational Facebook Posts That People Seem to Like 95

Chapter 12: People That Inspire Me and Closing
    Thoughts..112
Epilogue..118
Bonus Chapter: Post-Pandemic, Incredible Hardships
    and Incredible Opportunities to Respond Well and
    Refocus Your Energy Toward Your Dreams........121

Endorsement

"Hello there." (Had to say it.) I've only known Ricky Borba a short time, but within that time, I've come to find one of the most energetic, enthusiastic, and Christ-centered people I've ever met. We came to know each other because of my work in a studio, a long time ago, in a galaxy far, far away; however, we rarely talk about that. Our conversations are about creative endeavors and how they can best serve God's kingdom work.

The book you're about to read is no different. You'll be drawn in by Ricky's fun and unique take on his life, but moved to a deeper level by the sometimes tragic, sometimes revelatory ways the Lord has used and spoken to him. Back in 2013, I wrote a book called *JAT 365: 365 Daily Inspirations for the Pursuit of Your Dreams*. Yes, it's available on Amazon; yes, that's a shameless plug. In it, I touch on some of the same things Ricky does here in his book, and that is

best summed up by the words of C.S. Lewis who said, "You are never too old to set another goal or to dream a new dream." I suppose most things we say these days are summed up better by Mr. Lewis, but his writing inspired mine, and clearly has touched the soul of Ricky because we are both dreamers who, by the grace of God, have been able to turn our dreams into goals, and our goals into achievements. It's my deepest prayer that Ricky's book would help you accomplish the same. Dreams, goals are important in the recipe of our lives, but also realizing that resistance is a huge part of actually attaining them. So as you endeavor to read this concise, yet potent book, remember that Ricky's dreams and goals were always met head-on with two things: 1) a challenge or hurdle, and 2) God's ever-loving, compassionate hand that rested on his shoulder at the right time, even when he didn't feel it or believe it. The Lord is holding each one of us. It is up to us to let go and simply rest in His embrace. I challenge you, as you read, to make notes, to pray, to breathe, but most importantly, allow Christ to speak in the places that feel unattainable or void. He has never let me down, He has always answered my cries, and it has always been on His terms, which are so much better than I could ever try and control through my own will.

So in my best movie trailer announcer voice, which, yes, you've probably heard at some point, "In a world where one man will try to inspire and transform the heart of even one soul, get ready for an action-packed, edge of your seat, non-stop, pulse-pounding thrill ride!" Okay, I may have gone a little over-the-top, but you will be blessed by this piece of Ricky's heart and soul laid out to inspire and motivate you. As the voice of Obi-Wan Kenobi for over two decades, I'd be remiss if I didn't end this with, "May the fork be with you"...no wait, that's not it, anyway,

God bless and may His force be with you, always.

James Arnold Taylor
Actor/Entertainer (*Star Wars: The Clone Wars*)

Prologue to the Prologue

Ever read a book with two prologues before? Me either. But this is my book and they tell me I can do pretty much anything I want! So, I'm writing a prologue to my original prologue! The original prologue was written at 11:20am, July 28th, 2014. I checked the creation date of the Word doc for this book.

I am writing this proprologue (or would it be prologuelogue?) on July 10th, 2023! Which also happens to be my brother Danny's birthday. Happy birthday Danny! I think you're 41 today., You have a LOT more gray hair than me, for me being almost five years older than you. I'd say sorry, but we both know I'm not. Moving on…

A LOT has happened in my life in the almost nine years to the day since I began writing this book! Here's a quick rundown, in random order. We moved from Sacramento CA to Nashville TN and bought our first house.

We added two more kids to the family, bringing the grand total of children to five. I've directed three movies, two went into theaters, one of them was in the top ten box office and my upcoming fourth and fifth movies will be shot within months of each other this year! I've grown in my relationship with the Lord. I've ridden almost 4000 miles on my bicycle. I've made new friends, lost some old ones. I've started wearing reading glasses in bed at night when I'm on my phone. And now that I've depressed myself with that last sentence, I think I'll stop.

I started writing this book because God put it on my heart to do so. He knew that if I remained in Him and kept pushing forward, that I would begin to realize some of the dreams and desires that HE put in my heart and mind. And by golly, in the last nine years quite a few of them have come to fruition. As I'm sitting here in my Nashville home, looking at the movie posters of films I've directed and awards received for those films (which honestly don't add any value to my life, but it is nice to know my peers like my work) I could die a happy, content, fulfilled man right now. In terms of a paycheck God has GROSSLY overpaid me in my life.

See. One of the things I've learned in these nine years from my mentor and spiritual father Francis Anfuso, whom I talk a little about in Chapter 11 (no not that chapter 11. He's not bankrupt), is that I am the CEO of the Respond Well Department of my life. I say it so much that my kids want to hurt me when I say it to them at this point. But there have been so many bumps, bruises, twists, turns, false starts, non-starts and so forth the last nine years, that had I not had that phrase seared into my inner being, I honestly probably would have quit. But I kept going, and now in the rearview mirror, everything looks incredible. I try not to look ahead because that road is filled with obstacles and "impossibilities" that seem insurmountable.

So, as you read this book of mine, there will be spots where there seems to be some big-time jumps. And that's because over nine years, I wrote this book in chunks as things started to progress in my career and life. I sat down on July 28th, 2014, with a dream from the Lord and absolutely no idea how I'd get there. But I knew God wanted me to share this journey with people at that moment in time, before I "made it" (whatever that means). And, as of right now, I have no idea where my dreams and career are going to take me. Because like I said, I could die a very happy and content man right now, and not feel like I was sold a "Bill of Goods" by God. Meaning, I've now done things beyond my wildest dreams in terms of my career.

I'm excited for you to read this book. Really. I've shared it with a few people prior to getting it published, and it really does seem to have the ability for the reader to be able rerack and focus back on God. There are going to be some testimonials from people who have read the book on the following pages, and my hope is that their words will encourage you even more than my own.

So sit back, relax, put your readers on, get a marker or a pen (you're going to need them) and prepare to have a reading experience like you've never had before! Literally, because you've never read this book so it's truly a new experience. And if you're reading this book for second or third time, look closely at this dot for seven seconds, and your mind will be wiped so that it will be like you're reading it for the first time.

Prologue

The great thing about my book (at the time of this writing) is that I'm not sitting here writing from my hilltop mansion, with a Ferrari in the driveway, and two manservants waiting on me. Okay. Maybe that's extreme. I actually don't know anyone with a hilltop mansion. (I did when I was growing up, but that will come later). I do know someone with a Ferrari, though. My brother's boss. Swell guy. Drives a Ferrari. Okay, back to my point. I'm not writing this book from the vantage point of "Look at my success. Here's how to achieve what I have. Keep reading."

No, I'm in the middle of my pursuit. Truth be told, at the time of this writing, I am 36 years old and I don't have what most people would consider success. My car is from 1992. My wife's car is from 2001. We rent. We don't have a 401k, a stock portfolio, or anything resembling a retirement fund. We live check to check. And more times than not, there's more month than money. Some months the rent is paid late. Very late. We owe more money to student loans right now than I care to even keep writing about. Let's just say that between my wife's chiropractic degree, and my pastoral/theology degree, we owe more than what the president makes a year. Well, *on the books*, anyway. I don't know what he makes in addition to his salary. I have three daughters, two dogs and the vast majority of my kids' clothes are hand-me-downs. About the nicest thing I own is my TV. I LOVE my TV. See, I'm a filmmaker, so having a nice TV is important for editing and other work-related things. (That's what I tell my wife, anyway. So far so good. She hasn't questioned it.)

I would like to acknowledge, however, that despite our financial situation, the fact that I live in California, rent a house, own two cars, have food in my fridge, clothes on my back and in my closet, and that we earn a living that provides for every need we have, makes me a very "rich" man. I get that. My point was that in terms of what most people look to define success as, we aren't there. We are working towards it, and with God's help, I believe I will leave a legacy for my children and their children and their children. That is if Jesus hasn't decided to wrap things up by then.

So. Back to this book into. My hope and prayer is that as you read this book God put on my heart to write, you begin to take steps to pursue your passions and dreams and that your faith grows deeper as you begin to put that into motion. Who knows, maybe by the time you read this, I'll be acting or directing my first feature-length film, and you can tell your friends that you read my book when I was a nobody. Actually, acting in a film doesn't make me a someone. My identity is solely tethered to Christ, and that's where I get my sense of self-worth. And it's my hope and prayer that by the end of this book, it's where you get yours too.

CHAPTER 1

God is in the Business of Showing Off and He Wants to Show Off Through YOU

Song for this chapter:
Hall and Oates – *You Make My Dreams Come True*

Nine plus years ago when I began writing this book, every word in the prologue was true. (I hadn't written the prologue to the prologue yet, but it is also true.) I was chasing my dream and believing God's calling for my life, but really had no idea how all of that was going to come to be. I just knew (based on my faith and a dream the Lord gave me) that my dreams would eventually come true someday. Now, as I sit here in the middle of finishing this book, things are quite a bit different than they were when I began writing. Let me fill you in. Buckle up, it's a roller coaster.

Also, side note: This was originally chapter nine. Then after my friend read the manuscript he suggested that THIS chapter become the first chapter because he thought that it started the book off with more of a personal touch than the original chapter one, which is now chapter two. And because I respect him and his thought process, I shifted things around which took like a WHOLE HOUR. My grandfather built cabinets. I had to copy and paste some things around in a Word document. Both of those tasks require the same amount of energy and labor in my opinion.[1]

Okay, now I'll get to the meat of the story in an effort to keep myself on point. I tend to be a little long-winded at times. So here goes... At the end of 2016, which was about two years after I had begun writing this book, a script came along my way, and I felt it would be a great film to make up here in my neck of the woods, and it could be done relatively cheap if we were smart about it. So I took it to my guys and we all decided we should give it a shot. We knew we needed a couple of names to "sell the film" once it was done, so we began putting our thinking caps on as to who those two guys could be. I had mentally made up my mind that two actors I'd

---

[1] I've never made a cabinet before so I really don't know what I'm talking about.

grown up watching would be perfect for the two main roles. So, I looked them up and found out that both of them were managed by the same person. Now, I'm a guy that, for better or worse, is pretty bold. So I decided to email this producer/manager and ask him if we could get these two guys for our film. He said yes, and a couple of non-refundable deposits later, we had these two guys attached.

"Excitement filled the air," as they say. I met up with one of the actors who was doing a local autograph show, and we cut a few promos and laid out the plans for our crowd-funding campaign to finance this film. Well, without getting into details, that effort blew up in our faces through absolutely no fault of our own. We had spent months building the campaign, building the audience, and doing our due diligence on how to actually produce a film the right way. Needless to say, I was **extremely** upset when it fell through. And to be fair, I didn't handle it awesomely. I kind of griped and moaned about it to anyone that would listen. Woe was me.

About a week later, I drove to the Bay Area to do some work to earn some extra income. It was my daughter's birthday. Her party and dinner started at 5 in Sacramento, which meant I needed to leave the bay area no later than 2 p.m. Thankfully, I was able to do just that, and head out of town. But, about thirty minutes into my drive, I realized there was a bridge I was going to have to cross to get home, and I didn't have the $7 bridge toll to do so. (Out in California, you can't pay bridge tolls with your debit card. It's either cash, or you need a device in your car that the bridge senses when you drive over it, and it debits your bank account. Well, I don't drive to the Bay Area often enough to warrant that device, so I always just bring cash with me.) I realized I needed to pull off and find an ATM machine so I can pull $20 out to pay my bridge toll. I opened my phone and looked for the closest ATM, and it was a good 10 minutes off the freeway exit. (Don't judge me. It was almost stop and go traffic, so it wasn't like I was driving 75 mph while looking down at my phone, mmkay?) I realized that if I were to pull off and go to that ATM, I would be at a minimum 25 minutes off my ETA to my daughter's party, and possibly longer, considering how bad traffic was getting.

So I did what any other normal thinking person would do. I kept driving toward the tollbooth. And while I was driving toward the tollbooth, I started getting upset about the whole film fallout again. I'm trying to keep this book PG, so I'll just say I had a very colorful prayer to God. (By the way, I really don't think God minds when we pray like that. He's big enough and loves us enough to hear our hearts even if we're using what some would consider inappropriate language. #controversialstatement) Not only was I getting upset, I decided in my anger and disappointment that I was going to do what I had been told by many pastors and teachers not to do, which was throw a fleece out to God. The final words of my prayer went something like this. "God, I'm so tired of things not coming together in terms of my career, that I honestly feel like giving up sometimes. This being one of those times. SO, if you are INDEED behind this film and ME as a filmmaker, I *NEED* the person ahead of me to pay my bridge toll so I know you're with me on this dream you've given me." (Somewhere all my pastors and teachers are cringing while reading this.)

I pulled up to the bridge toll booth, and because my car was so awesome, the driver's side window wouldn't roll down. So I opened my door, I looked at the bridge toll guy and I said "Look, I don't have any cash, I'm really sorry." He said, and I will never EVER forget it, **"Don't worry, that car ahead of you paid for your toll."** Talk about a watershed moment in my life. I'm actually crying right now just typing this out, remembering what I felt in that moment.

I couldn't believe it. I really couldn't. And after a few seconds of me looking like I'd seen a ghost, with tears streaming down my face, I closed my car door on that 2001 Ford Escape, and drove as fast as that car would go, to catch up to the car ahead of me that paid my toll. I pull up next to it, honking my horn to get their attention, and the sweetest looking elderly African American couple looked over at me and smiled. But that wasn't good enough for me. So, I began SCREAMING, "THANK YOU! THANK YOU! THANK YOU! YOU HAVE NO IDEA WHAT THIS MEANS!" The guy driving the car looked at me like, "Dude, it's no big deal, it was just seven bucks." But I just kept saying thank you over and over again while crying like a newborn.

I don't remember the ride home after that. I just remember getting to the restaurant in Roseville where my wife and kids and her parents were waiting for me, and barely being able to get that story out fast enough. My wife and her parents both started crying when they heard me tell it, and to this day, I would give my left arm to know the names of those two people whose random act of kindness was an answer to my prayer.

From that day forward, I decided I was never going to feel sorry for myself or doubt God again. That no matter what, I would stay the course, follow my dreams, be content with whatever life threw at me, and respond better to things when they didn't go my way.

Fast forward now. About a month later, a person I had met briefly at a film festival called me and told me he had a friend who invested in indie films, and that I should drive down and meet him in Beverly Hills to talk about my film because he was interested in it after hearing my friend pitch it to him. So I did just that. I hopped in a rental car, drove to Beverly Hills, and pitched this investor this film, and he agreed to finance it. I was elated. The manager of the two actors was there too, as we had brought him on board to help produce the film. It all felt like a dream come true. I was finally on my way.

Or was I.

Without getting into details, the process of getting the film funded was a process that most people had warned me not to do. But my team and I vetted this guy and decided we were comfortable enough to go through the procedures and hoops he had put forth in order to get the film funded. Long story short, about three months after we did all of the things he asked for, we found out that it was all an elaborate misdirection. We were absolutely never going to be funded by this person, and the time, money, and effort we put into doing all the things he asked us to do were not going to be reimbursed or returned. We had fallen prey to someone people had warned us about, and it was our own fault.

I decided to not just put on my best face, but to actually live that out. Those six months in dealing with him and going through location scouting, casting, etc., had taught me invaluable lessons, lessons you can really only learn in the fire. Not the types of things you can learn from books or masterclasses. (By the way, I LOVE masterclasses. Well worth the money to take those online courses from famous people in their specific fields.) I chose to remember the bridge toll, the promises God shared in my heart, the dreams He gave me, etc. I chose to remain happy and hopeful. Then, it happened. About four months after everything had blown up in our faces, the manager of those two actors, who ultimately came aboard to help us produce that film, called me. It was on October 4th. Exactly one week shy of the one-year anniversary of the bridge toll day. I was pulling into Burger King. (Chicken sandwiches from Burger King are my favorite. I would eat them every day, every meal if I could.) He said, "Look, my business partner and I think you're just about the most positive person we've ever met. We can't understand how you've remained so upbeat during the last few months. So in that, we've decided that we want to offer you the job of VP of Film in our film production company based here in Los Angeles. You wouldn't have to move or anything, but we would love to have you come aboard and give you first right of refusal to direct any film that comes our way that you feel comfortable with."

I was quite literally speechless. I also began crying a bit. (Being a father of four girls and a boy will do that to a man.) I happily accepted the new job and began feeling an incredible amount of joy come over me. Then he said, "We have this film called *The Talking Tree* that we think you'd be perfect for. It's faith-based and tear-jerker." He then let me know that it wasn't funded, but that if I wanted to direct it, it was mine. He sent the script that day, and I read it that night. It was a really beautifully written script. It was about a man in his 40's who finds out his mother (whom he is extremely close to) has stage 3 cancer. So he robs a bank to pay for her medical bills and gets caught. He goes to jail and the rest of the movie is "Will he get out of prison in time to see his mother before she passes?"

I liked it a lot. I really did. But I didn't love it. It was lacking something for me that I couldn't put my finger on. But that was in no way going to deter me from directing that film. So, I WHOLE-heartedly accepted their offer of directing that film and began seeking out investors for it. I had met with a couple of friends of mine who invested in film, to see if they were interested in making a small investment so that we could go into pre-production, but they both politely declined. I was disappointed but kept at it.

Months later, my wife and I give birth to our fourth child, Caden. My first and only son. It was July 6th, 2017. We were elated. My sister, my wife's entire family, many of our friends and my own mother were there that day. My mom, who always goes above and beyond, had actually come in the day before and rented a hotel room near the hospital so she could be closer to us and stay longer, as her house was a good two hours away. The next day, July 7th, was my wife's ~~redacted~~th birthday. My mom had gone to a few stores, gotten a cake and some presents for my wife, and we celebrated the birth of my son and my wife's birthday that day. The next day my mom didn't come by the hospital, but she called to let us know she'd be by the next day because she felt like she was passing a kidney stone, even though it didn't really hurt as they did normally. The next day my wife and I drove home and settled in with our new baby and three older girls.

Then my mom called. "I took an MRI and they don't like what they see in my liver." We prayed and then started talking about the baby. It didn't feel like it was a moment. It felt like, okay, well, whatever it is, you'll be fine. Now, I don't remember the exact passage of time here, but the next phone call I got from my mom was one I'll never forget. "Stage IV liver cancer. It's in my bones too." It didn't feel like a truck hit me, but I did sit down in order to compose myself. My wife, however, being in the medical field, did not like what she heard, and broke down immediately.

Seven weeks later, my mother was dead. Cancer had taken her life in less than two months.

This is by far my least favorite thing to talk about, write about, or think about. And despite the fact that I KNOW my mother is in heaven, it still hurts horribly, two years later. Having said that…..Genesis 50:20, in the RBRV (Ricky Borba Revised Version), says that when the $#*& hits the fan, God has a plan. (I know, I know. It literally says "What the devil intended for harm, God will use for good.")

Remember earlier when I said I didn't love the script for *The Talking Tree*? (By the way, *The Talking Tree* got renamed to *Hope for the Holidays*. It's on Amazon. Go watch it, please.) Looking back, what I didn't love was the dialogue and interactions between the main character and his mom. I could tell it was written by someone who hadn't gone through what they were writing about. So, with the permission of the writer, and with the permission of the producer of the film, I went and rewrote every single line that the mother speaks in the film. Not only THAT, but I rewrote all of those lines as DIRECT quotes from my own mother as she was going through her battle with cancer.

I was able to turn *Hope for the Holidays* into a love letter to my mother. I don't know how many children get to honor their parents in such a beautiful and unique way, but let me promise you, it was not and is not lost on me that THIS film was my first film and that I was able to use my experience with my mother to make this film feel more authentic. Not only that, but an Oscar-nominated actress ended up playing the role of my mother. Seriously! So, imagine my utter joy, heartache, and happiness watching Sally Kirkland deliver lines in a film that my own mother said to me in real life. As someone who loves film and storytelling, I couldn't have written something better for myself. If my mom was going to die of cancer, what better way to honor her than to make a film that will touch lives for years to come, using her own words. I'm in awe about it. God truly does care about us, and His words are absolutely true.

My hope and prayer are that you don't have to go through what I went through with my mom in order for your dreams to come true. But I do pray that whatever bumps you encounter on the road to your dreams, you're able to see how God is using them to your benefit.

I need to back up for a second because I got ahead of myself a bit there. There was a reason I mentioned my couple of investor friends who politely declined to invest in the film. My mom passed away around 11 p.m. on September 3rd, 2017. I got a phone call around 8 a.m. on September 4th, (2017 obviously) from one of my two friends. He is not on social media and had no idea my mother had passed, by the way. He started the call off by saying, "Hey Ricky, I know we haven't spoken in a few months, but something woke me up around 1 a.m. and told me I needed to invest in your film. So, I'm obeying what I believe is an urging from the Lord, and I want to invest such and such an amount toward *The Talking Tree*." I probably looked whiter than a sheet of paper with a flashlight shining on it. I said, "Scott, do you know how much this means to me right now? My mom passed away less than 12 hours ago." At that point, he and I were both in tears.

With that money, we were able to kick *Hope for the Holidays* into pre-production. From there, one of my two investment friends hooked me up with the man that would eventually finance the entire film. The rest, as they say, is history. Fourteen months later we were on set for the first day of shooting the actual film, and I sat in my director's chair for the very first time—a chair my mother had bought me ten years ago as a Christmas gift because she too, believed in my dreams.

By the way, I'm okay if you end up watching *Hope for the Holidays* and not liking it. (Although I would be majorly surprised by that because it is an incredible film, if I do say so myself.) I will NOT, however, be okay with YOU if you don't like what the character of Georgia has to say in the film. Her words are my mom's words. K? K.

As of the writing of this book, that was three years ago, and *Hope for the Holidays* was put out to the masses that year. I literally couldn't wait for the world to see it. Shortly after, the producer of *Hope for the Holidays* moved up to Sacramento from Los Angeles, and he and I opened a film office in the Sacramento region. It all happened so fast my head spun, especially considering how long it took to get all of it going.

The old adage is true: when God opens a door, no one can close it. Right now the door feels wide open, especially since moving to Nashville in January of 2022.

CHAPTER 2

Identity

**Song to accompany this chapter:
Linkin Park – *The Catalyst***

Before you go chasing your dreams, you need to know who you are first, so you know where you're going. If I were a fish and didn't understand that oxygen could kill me, it wouldn't be prudent (not at this juncture) for me to set out on a Forrest Gump-like run across the states. I have to know who I am first before I start down the road of making my dreams come true. (We will unpack dreams and how they relate to God's calling in your life later in this book, btw.) (Also, if you want an entire book devoted to this topic, I highly recommend Mark Driscoll's *Who Do You Think You Are?* And if, like me, money is somewhat tight, you can listen to about 10 weeks' worth of sermons Mark did on his book here: https://realfaith.com/sermon-series/who-do-you-think-you-are/

We like to use Psalm 139:13 a lot, don't we? We like to remind ourselves that God created our inmost being while in our mother's womb. But when was the last time you read the next five verses? They are amazing! And I don't use that word flippantly. I can't stand it when people declare everything is amazing. How's that Burger King chicken sandwich, Pete? Amazing. What did you think of that community theater play, Crystal? Amazing. Seen the new smartphone OS?! It's AMAZING. See what I'm getting at here? No. Those things aren't amazing. Did that chicken sandwich cause great surprise and sudden wonder? Not unless it had a diamond in it. Did that community theater play where ¾ of the people in it forgot their lines astonish you? Most likely, no. That's why it's community theater. But when you look at Psalm 139:14-18, those verses ARE amazing. Those verses DO astonish me and cause sudden wonder. To think that God has not only made me but ordained my days is frankly overwhelming. In other words, God has predestined our days. He's got plans for them. So it would seem fitting that we try and stick to *His* plan.

Have you ever done an online search for "Who does God say I am?" Go ahead. Do it now. This book will be here when you get back. I promise. Go. Now.

Wait. I guess I should take into consideration that some of you might "suck at the internet", so here's a link you can copy and paste to a good search result I found: https://bible.org/article/who-does-god-say-i-am

It's pretty fascinating what the Bible says about who God says you are. Problem is, we have sensory overload telling us otherwise. The music we listen to, shows and movies we watch, billboards we see, people we choose to let speak in our lives, the clothes we wear, cars we drive, the status of our bank accounts, what our friends post on social media, and on and on and on (till the break a break a dawn) pound our minds into submission, making us believe we are not who God says we are. (For a fascinating look into what and how culture shapes how we feel about ourselves, watch this: http://www.pbs.org/wgbh/pages/frontline/shows/cool/view/)

Let's say we are "good Christians" and spend 30 minutes reading our Bible every day. That's roughly three hours a week. Let's add another hour or so of church. Now we're at four hours. And if you're into that sort of thing, let's say you listen to Christian music almost exclusively. (Why someone would listen to Christian music almost exclusively is beyond me, but hey, to each their own) Now we're somewhere in the four-to-eight-hour range per week, of being infused with time spent with identity-affirming information going into our brains. But, according to a study at the University of California, San Diego, by 2015, the sum of media asked for and delivered to consumers on mobile devices and to their homes would take more than 15 hours a day to see or hear. That volume is equal to 6.9 million-million gigabytes of information, or a daily consumption of nine DVDs worth of data per person per day. (http://ucsdnews.ucsd.edu/pressrelease/u.s._media_consumption_to_rise_to_15.5_hours_a_day_per_person_by_2015) That's 15.5 hours a DAY. We just deduced that we get about four to eight hours a WEEK if we are intentional about our quiet times and positive media consumption. I'm no math wizard, but when you put four to eight hours up against 108.5, it's no wonder we have such a self-esteem and self-worth epidemic worldwide. You can't win a battle against this type of thing when the percentages are almost 99% to 1%. It's almost impossible. *Almost.*

You have to be proactive. Not reactive. Tony Dungy said that "a goal without a plan is a wish." If you're hoping to change or secure your identity in Christ, or even just get a more positive outlook on yourself, you need to be devoting time and coming up with a *plan* to start skewing the percentages the other way.

Since this is my book, I'll use myself as an example. From literally the time I can remember, I've absolutely loved being the center of attention. I remember doing a commercial for my cousin's senior class when I was five. I remember how it felt when I was eight and took the stage for the first time. I remember summers in my grandparents' backyard, standing on top of the pool filter box, singing "It Takes Two" by Rob Base and DJ EZ-

Rock and watching my entire family stop swimming to see what craziness I was going to come up with. I made my first film at 12 years old on my parent's VHS Camcorder (when you had to edit IN CAMERA!) By 18, I had an agent in San Francisco, and was doing commercials all over the bay area. At 24, I beat out all other comers to land the lead role on a nationally televised syndicated show on the WB Network. So. What's so important about any of that, Ricky? What's important, reader, is that I've known what makes me tick from the time I can remember. I didn't grow up wondering what I wanted to do with my life. I knew I wanted to act in, write and direct films. But you know, a funny thing happened on the way to the forum. I also realized I was good with computers. Without any school, I understood how operating systems worked and how to fix the majority of PC related problems. And since living in the Bay Area is expensive, and acting doesn't exactly pay the bills roun' those parts, guess what kinds of jobs I found myself doing more and more of? That's right. Sitting behind a desk, taking phone calls helping people fix their computer problems. Not a SHRED of creativity involved in that. But hey, it paid the bills (mostly) and no one could say I was being foolish. (More on what people will tell you about yourself later.)

I remember being depressed (not clinically) because I wasn't fulfilling any of my desires. I NEED to have a creative outlet. That's who *I* am. Unfortunately, somewhere along the way, I decided that my needs and passion were secondary and tertiary (I learned that word in college. I try and use it as often as possible because it makes me sound smart) to what I thought I wanted my life to look like. Problem was, I had NO idea at the time that chasing your dreams was just about the MOST Godly thing I could do. God doesn't want us miserable 40 hours a week. If we are supposed to be representing Him at the workplace, how can we represent Him well if we don't even like ourselves when we are there? There's ~~no~~ *hardly any* opportunity to witness to others when we are miserable. When you are in your element, whatever that is for you, how do you feel? Put the book down right now and put yourself in your querencia. (It's a Spanish slang word for "home or sanctuary." That place you go that resonates with you. I learned this word in Mrs. Mattingly's 11th grade English class. If you have a problem with it, take it up with her.) Are you in your querencia in your mind yet? Where are you? What's around you? What are you doing? How are you feeling right now? Pretty "amazing," right? Imagine if that place you're thinking of was the place you spent the vast majority of your time. For me, it's a film set. For my wife, it's her chiropractic office. For my two-year-old son, it seems to be in the one area of the backyard we've told him not to go.

Here's another example from my life I'll use to illustrate this point, the point of choosing a vocation in step with your identity. I have an uncle who loves rock and roll music like no one I've ever known. He has LP's (you see, kids, LPs are what people used to listen to music on. They're also commonly referred to as records) stacked from the floor to the ceiling, 12-15 feet wide. There isn't a band he hasn't heard of or a song he doesn't know the lyrics to. Rock and roll music is his querencia. To this day, he still goes to concerts and can tell incredible stories about attending concerts for hall of fame rockers in the '60s and '70s *before* they even came out with their first album. As he's told me a few times, his dream growing up was to own a record store. I mean why WOULDN'T that be his dream?! Sell records, have rock stars come to your store to drive business, get free tickets to concerts all the time, the list goes on and on!

My uncle also happens to love God. He always has. He was raised that way, and he raised his kids that way, and his kids are raising their kids that way. He's a good man. A moral, giving, loving and devoted man. I guess back in his "formative years" though, he decided that owning a record store wasn't a wise decision. I would have to assume that back in the '60s, he saw working his way up the corporate ladder was the most sensible way to take care of his family, and he did just that. He is leaving a legacy for his children and their children and their children's children. Not just a financial legacy, either. He's leaving the most important legacy a man *can* leave his family, and that's faith in Christ.

However.

His story breaks my heart when I look at it through the lens of his God-ordained days. Instead of selling records at his corner store, he was sitting at a desk crunching numbers and traveling overseas to make sure the corporation's widgets were in order. Can I say emphatically that God wanted something different for his life? No. But I can imagine what kind of witness he would have been to all those people who would have walked into his store to purchase a rock and roll album. Imagine a Christian man who loves rock and roll being given the opportunity to share about himself to people who more than likely don't know God. (Pump your brakes. I'm not saying people who like rock and roll are in need of redemption. Not at all. I'm just making the point that more than likely the majority of people who would have walked through his doors would have been non-Christians.) Imagine the guy who walked in to buy an album, who wasn't a Christian, finding out that the record store owner attended a church up the road?! That Christians weren't just judgmental hatemongers who hated rock and roll! Imagine the impact my uncle could have had if he had chased his dream and opened that record store! Sure, he may not have been as financially successful, but imagine how many lives he would have touched with his love for rock music and love for God all coming to a head!

See, it's not even enough to *know* your identity. If you don't do things that express who you are at your core, then the only things you will express are frustration unfulfillment. You have to act out of your identity. YOU have to because there is no one else like YOU to make up the slack. YOU are uniquely gifted and qualified to go forth in YOUR area of passion. No two painters, drummers, hot dog stand owners or tax attorneys are alike. YOUR mark will be drastically different than someone else even in your same field.

Try for the next few moments to clear your mind of all the things this world has told you about who you are. Try to go back to that day when you were little, playing outside, and you were pretending to be a _____. What's the blank? Fill it in. It's your book. You bought it. You can write in it all you want. You can even rip pages out if you want. Go ahead. There are blank pages at the end of this book. Rip them out.

Feel good?! Good. Now fill this little questionnaire out. It's about who you are.

Thinking less of yourself is not humility; it's pride turned inside upon yourself. True humility is believing what God says about you is true. You are allowed to feel good about yourself. And don't worry about going too far with it. God will put you in your place if He needs to. This exercise is meant to AFFIRM who GOD says you are. Elohim is the Name given for God as the Creator of the universe. (Genesis 1:1-2:4a. Go read it. It's in the Bible. There's one on the bed over there.) The name Elohim implies strength, power, and justice. So, the God of the universe, ELOHIM, not only created the universe with strength, power, and justice but has created YOU in the same way. He has used various methods to tell you about yourself, whether it be through other people, prophetic word, a Bible verse that speaks to you, a skill you are good at, and so forth and so on and so forth and then some. God, the creator of the universe, is CRAZY about you and thinks you are ALL that AND a bag of chips. So go ahead and use this exercise to affirm yourself and to remind yourself that you are, in fact, someone special.

Make a list of non-spiritual things you're good at. We'll get to the spiritual things later.

_____
_____
_____
_____
_____
_____

I really love the way I _____

When people give you compliments, they say.......

_____
_____
_____
_____
_____
_____
_____

Other people think this stuff is hard, but not me. These are things that come naturally to me that don't necessarily come natural to others...........

_____
_____
_____
_____
_____
_____
_____

If I could clone myself and populate the earth entirely of my clones, the earth would be known for _____.

When it comes to relationships, I am really good at......

_____
_____
_____
_____
_____
_____

God likes to speak to us through many different avenues. Here are some of the ways God speaks to me:

_____
_____
_____
_____
_____
_____

God has spoken to me through the ways I just wrote down. Here are some of the things He's said:

_____
_____
_____
_____
_____
_____

God has gifted me with many spiritual gifts. Here are my top 29:

_____
_____
_____
_____
_____
_____
_____
_____

The Bible verse I'm attached to right now is _____, because God is telling me _____ through it.

Other people have affirmed me spiritually by telling me, writing me, texting me, sending me smoke signals and otherwise, that I...

_____
_____
_____
_____
_____
_____
_____

Finally, if "ME" were made into a movie,
the tagline of ME would be:
(here are some examples from famous movies)

The story of a man who was too proud to run.
High Noon

You'll believe a man can fly!
Superman

An adventure 65 million years in the making.
Jurassic Park

Fear can hold you prisoner. Hope can set you free.
The Shawshank Redemption

Life is like a box of chocolates…
you never know what you're gonna get.
Forrest Gump

Nothing is as simple as black and white.
Pleasantville

_____
_____
_____
_____

Look at you. You made it to the end of chapter 2. Doesn't it feel good? You accomplished something I've only done a few times, because I hate to read. Seriously, I've only read through the first couple chapters of about 10 books.

Hopefully, you're starting to develop a better sense of who you are at this point. Good. Because chapter 3 is all about trusting God to take care of you through the process of chasing your dreams. Ready? Go.

CHAPTER 3

Pressing into God, AKA: Trust

Song to accompany this chapter:
Scribble **by Underworld**

Without getting into every single detail of the dream, 10 years ago I had my first ever prophetic dream. To paint a picture of where I was at in my life, my wife was pregnant with our third child and we were homeless (the home we were renting went through a short-sale, and we were given eight days to move out), so we shacked up with a good friend of mine from college. (See, going to college later in life has its perks. People who are past their mid-20's possess this thing called "empathy." Anywhoooo...) it was our 10-year wedding anniversary, and to say I had a bad attitude about my life's circumstances on that night would be an understatement. I went to bed angry and frustrated with God for what I perceived to be Him dropping the ball on my life. My prayer that night was something to the effect of, "HEY! REMEMBER ME?! THE GUY YOU ASKED TO MOVE AWAY FROM HIS CHILDHOOD CITY TO A BRAND NEW CITY WHERE I KNOW NO ONE?! YEAH, THINGS AREN'T GOING SO GREAT. 'THANKS.'"

God heard that prayer and knew I was frustrated. How do I know? Because I had the most vivid, "amazingly" special dream I've ever had in my life. Long story short, God was communicating with me through a Bluetooth earpiece while I was on a military-style mission to make films. By the end of the dream, I was in my 70's and had made a lot of movies that had impacted the world.

Okay, now that we're clear on that, let me get to my point. That dream was 10 years ago and has at times **literally been the only thing** keeping me going in my pursuit of filmmaking. There have been SO many days, months, and even years that I've wanted to pack it in and call it quits on this whole filmmaking dream of mine. It's a very hard thing, following your dreams, especially when there's not really a roadmap to success that you can follow. So much of filmmaking is not "what you know, but who you know." Then when you consider the fact that I live in Sacramento and have never really made a name for myself in the industry, the task seems daunting.

The real temptation to quit following my dreams, though, is the fact that there is good money and a lot of opportunity to either work in technology (an area I'm gifted and have experience in) or to go work at a church. Along with those financial opportunities in doing those jobs, no one would ever question my decision to "play it safe" and go after either of those vocations. But, as I said in chapter 2, I know in my heart I would be absolutely miserable. I know I would literally hate every second of every day at either of those jobs. I would also feel guilty for "quitting on myself."

And that's the beauty of that dream that God gave me. He knew my spirit was willing but my flesh was weak. My prayer that night was sincere. I really was a mess. I really was upset. I really was considering giving up on myself. So God, in His infinite wisdom, gave me a dream that He knew would keep me motivated. And while the road to success hasn't been any easier since that dream, that dream did give me an unwavering stance on continuing to follow my dreams. I haven't doubted or wanted to give up on myself for one second since that dream. It's been the one thing keeping me going at times.

Okay, so enough about MY dream. This book is being written for YOUR dream. I'm sure as you've been reading this chapter the last few minutes (or few seconds, if you're one of those crazy speed-readers) that you've been thinking about your dreams. Maybe your dream is hard to obtain like mine. Maybe it's right in front of you, but for whatever reason, you're afraid of what others might think. Maybe you're afraid you'll fail. Maybe you're afraid you'll succeed. There are a lot of variables here. But the one thing I DO know is that YOUR dream is in YOUR heart for a reason. You were uniquely created. There is no one else on earth like you. Whatever dream you have, you are the ONLY person that can prevent it from happening! The biggest detractor from pursuing your dreams is self-doubt. So if this book does anything, I am hoping it removes some of the self-doubts so many of us suffer from.

Along with my dream keeping me going, there is also a Bible verse I have leaned heavily on during this pursuit. It's from the book of Matthew, chapter 6, in the "Do not worry" section of Jesus' Sermon on the Mount. (By the way, in my mind's eye, I always saw Jesus sitting on a rock with people surrounding Him on all sides during this sermon. I've never seen it in my mind as Him standing by himself on a stage and preaching down to everyone.) Verse 26 is the go-to verse for me. It states, "Look at the birds of the air; they do not sow or reap or store away in barns, and yet your heavenly Father feeds them. Are you not much more valuable than they? Can any one of you by worrying add a single hour to your life?" (NIV)

That verse gets me in the feels every time. It's so reassuring! My take on it is that Jesus is telling us that no matter WHAT, we can ALWAYS count on God to provide the basics for us. Food, shelter, clothes. So with that promise in mind, I've always told myself that at the very least, in pursuing my dreams, God **promises** that He'll clothe, feed, and provide shelter for me. And guess what, so far so good. You see, when you allow God to be God, meaning you take Him at His word and believe whole-heartedly that He won't lie to you or let you down, it gives you the freedom to live your life boldly. Not jump out of an airplane without a parachute type bold, but the type of boldness that removes fear and frustration from your life.

Let's face it. A lot of what motivates us in life is fear-based. There's a popular phrase among millennials nowadays, which is FOMO, or "fear of missing out." It's why an event like the Fyre Festival was able to get as much traction and media coverage as it did, despite the fact that it was a total sham. (If you don't know what the Fyre Festival was, you can watch it on Netflix here: https://www.netflix.com/title/81035279. There's also a documentary on Hulu about it.) In the day and age of social media, the temptation to "covet thy neighbor's wife, ox, car, house, etc." is at an all-time high. For example, my wife and I allow my daughter to have an Instagram account. We heavily monitor who she follows and the comments she receives, but already at this young age, we noticed that she was starting to become jealous of all her friends' posts. One friend was at Disneyland. Another was at the beach. A group of friends was at the movies together. It goes on and on. But what my daughter didn't understand until I explained it to her, was that these moments in life posted to Instagram aren't real. They aren't true. They're not honest. They're just moments. In the midst of your most difficult day, you could theoretically post a smiling selfie to Instagram and trick everyone into thinking your day was amazing. So, I pointed out to my daughter two things. First and foremost, we are never to be jealous of anyone else's success or good times. On the contrary, we should be happy for them and applaud them. But more importantly, I explained to my daughter what was truly important in life. God. Family. Friends. Things of that nature. Then it happened. After having a sit-down talk with her about this, she confided in me that most of her friends on Instagram who post the kinds of pictures where they're out and about at Disneyland or on vacations come from broken homes. She went down her friends list and pointed out over half of her friends that lived with only one of their parents because of divorce. It was an incredibly sad and simultaneously teachable moment for her.

    The fear when it comes to chasing your dreams is multi-layered. Failure. Finances. Loss of friends and or family because they think you're crazy or illogical.

Those are just a few of the fears I dealt with in pursuing my dreams, so I'm assuming they have to be some of the same fears that others face. But. (There's always a but!) In allowing yourself to let God's promises reign supreme in your heart and your mind, the number one side-effect is that fear is removed from your life! When you wake up **knowing** God not only is holding up His end of the bargain but **wants to** because He's a good father, the kind of freedom you gain is not something easily described.

Maybe there isn't anyone in your life you can look to for proof of this concept. But I'm here to tell you that I'm living proof. My life is an example of God providing for every single one of my needs as I pursued the dreams He's given me. However, I do want to be clear about something. The removal of fear in your life as you press into God more does not remove hardships. As much as we want those two things to happen simultaneously (fear going bye-bye and things getting easier), they don't often happen at the same time. And even though I hate to admit it, I'm actually glad they don't. Here's why. If you were given a winning lottery ticket without ever having learned to manage money properly, you would undoubtedly blow through all those winnings with nothing to show for it. There are a few principles here that I think stand out, the first being that if there was no resistance, or "difficulty" for lack of a better term, we wouldn't grow spiritually, mentally or physically. A while back, something struck me when I heard it, and it's helped me keep this principle near to my mind and heart. It is this: when astronauts return to earth after prolonged trips to space, the lack of resistance (gravity) in space causes their muscles to atrophy. That's why when you see footage of astronauts emerging from their vehicles after they touch down, they all look like baby giraffes trying to walk for the first time. There's a benefit to resistance, and it's that our muscles, minds, and souls will grow. Without it, we would remain in the same form physically, mentally, and spiritually.

And that's what pressing in is all about: developing spiritual muscle. When you press in and trust God, wonderful things happen. Things you weren't expecting. Things you prayed about long ago but had forgotten about. Things that not only last a lifetime but eternity. So as this chapter comes to a close, take a minute to do something for yourself. Turn your phone off. Shut down all distractions. Go find a quiet place, and then pray. Get on your knees. Pray earnestly. The book of James says that when we pray, we should pray with confidence because God likes that. So pray confidently that God will take care of you on this journey, all of your needs and some of your wants, and pray He will get you across that finish line, because He who started a good work will finish it! Pray! Now! I'll do it with you. Ready? GO.

CHAPTER 4

How Are You Defining Success?

Song to accompany chapter:
Beyond the Blue **by Josh Garrels**

Right off the bat, I'm going to tell you that there are books, articles, and other forms of media that discuss this topic better than I'm about to. "How you define success" is a critical element to one's life, because how you define success plays into so many other areas of your life. The most important thing it seems to define, though, is your happiness. One of the toughest lessons I've ever learned in my life is that my happiness is not and should not be based on my circumstances, but my perspective. Unfortunately, in this day and age, happiness is defined by what we own, how much we have in the bank, what's going on in our lives, etc. For me, I've made a concerted effort to let my perspective on what God thinks about me, my relationships with others, and my perspective on my future define my happiness, and that has made ALL the difference in the world. If you don't believe me, look no further than a news article from India in 2019. Over one million students took the country board of exams for high school. A computer glitch gave back very unfavorable results for the test, and because of that, 20 high school students committed suicide within a day of receiving their results. (https://www.foxnews.com/world/20-indian-students-commit-suicide-after-exam-results) What the underlying message of that story is, is that for those students, success was rolled into what their test results were. I can't imagine one of my children taking their own life, let alone doing it because of some score they got on a state test. We have to start redefining what success is! I want to spend this chapter rewiring how you define success for yourself, because I'm quite sure the vast majority of you aren't defining it the way God intended it to be defined.

One of my favorite pastors in the world, Mark Driscoll, puts it this way. Your net worth does not define your self-worth. Read that again. Socio-economic status does not define who you are one bit. To God. But I get it, it does matter to others. And that's hard and unnerving. It's difficult knowing that you're being judged based on superficial things like the clothes you're wearing or what car you're driving or if you were able to afford to go on that weekend trip with your friends or not.

Believe me, I've faced more judgment for being the age I am and having the lack of funds that I do. I've turned down more vacations, trips, and experiences than I can think of. The clothes I wear and the car I drive aren't anything to write home about (if writing home is still a thing?). It's been difficult at my age seeing the success of my friends, both older and younger, knowing "my ship" hasn't come in yet. But there's the rub. That's the problem right there. Did you catch it? I'm sure you did, because now I'm making a huge deal out of it. I was basing my "success" comparatively to what others around me have.

That in and of itself is a big problem, but there's an even bigger problem than that once you start going down the "grass is greener" road. And that is that you begin to lose sight of the wonderful things and blessings in your life. In only focusing on my net worth as my barometer, here are some of the things I became blind to, in no particular order: my health, my healthy children, my marriage, the food in my fridge, the roof over my head, running water, electricity, clothing, great friends, mostly supportive family members, all the talents and gifts God has given me, all my needs being met, and even some of my wants. I mean really, if I sat here and thought about it for more than two minutes, I could fill the rest of the pages of this book with things that I've been blessed with, that people who have the correct definition of success would agree make me successful. I've been to third-world countries. I know firsthand how fortunate I am to be an American living in the United States. But it's hard to keep that in focus. Every billboard, commercial, movie, and TV show constantly bombards us with the world's definition of success. They're constantly telling us that these materialistic things will bring us happiness. But the reality is, that's a lie. You can hop on Google right now and read any number of stories about a wealthy person taking their own life. There are multiple reasons for why this happens, but if you were to believe everything you see and hear about what money does for you, you'd walk away bewildered as to how anyone who is wealthy could be depressed, let alone take their own life. Your net worth does not define your self-worth.

So, what *does* define success? Are there any biblical passages that clearly lay this out? I believe there are. And oddly enough, I think the very first place you find one is in the book of Genesis. Before I unpack this, I'm going to do you a favor and give you the answer. I believe one of the ways God defines success is if you are being obedient to Him. When I read the account of Genesis, God is clearly happy with Adam and then Eve. (I mean, He loves Adam so much that he says "Here, here's someone you can be friends with and fall in love with, and oh, by the way, there's going to be a lot of physical pleasure to be had as well. Have fun, kids!") God gives them the run of the PLANET, save for one tree and one piece of fruit. They're free to do ANYTHING else they want except eat that fruit. Things are going great. Adam and Eve are naked 24/7. Literally, all of God's creation is in the palm of their hands. It's heaven on earth in every sense of the word. And then something happens. They disobey God and things change. God goes from totally proud of His kids to having Scotty beam Him down (energize!) to the garden so He can have a face to face with His kids. Adam and Eve were batting 1.000% up until that point. They were the definition of success. Then in one bite, failure entered the world and we have never been the same since. Disobedience is not part of the formula for success. It's impossible to be successful if you aren't obedient to the rules and way things are done to get you to the top of the mountain you're climbing. God came down to earth and had a little chat with His kids to let them know that moving forward, their disobedience was going to result in some pretty un-fun side effects. Toiling in your labor (I've always loved that phrase for some reason), birth-pains, etc. In fact, because of disobedience, we went from the creation of the first two humans to MURDER, in ONE generation.

So how does this apply to chasing your dreams and not giving up on yourself? I'm glad you asked. I believe we are most successful when we are pursuing God and the dreams He put in our hearts. When you read the Bible and make notes as to all the times God and Jesus are proud of their followers, you find that it almost always follows obedience. Think about it this way. Let's say you have a child. You tell your kid that you need them to clean up the backyard patio because you're having guests for dinner at 7, and everyone is eating outside. So, you leave for work in the morning and you come home expecting to find that patio clean and ready for guests. Only to find out that your kid either didn't do it at all or decided that doing something else entirely was most important. In this scenario, your kid just flat-out disobeyed you, which is going to have multiple ramifications. One, they're in trouble and can expect discipline. Two, the task you needed and wanted to be done isn't, resulting in either a change of plans, or you wasting time yourself fixing it. And three, you'll be reluctant to trust your kid with another task for the time being. All those principles apply to us when it comes to following our dreams.

If God has given you a dream to do something with your life (hint: He most certainly has), he is expecting you to do it! Why? Because it's in following THAT dream that will give you ultimate success! God has infinite wisdom and knows what's best for us. The dreams He's given each of us are dreams that are going to be most meaningful to US, the one He gave the dream to. Have you ever met someone who has had a taste of their dream coming true? It's infectious! Walk up to ANY professional athlete and ask them what the feeling was like the day they were drafted. Guaranteed they'll spend a minute or two trying to fight back tears as they recount the journey to get to that point, and the satisfaction they felt when their number was called. Ask any small business owner what it felt like the day they opened their business and their first customer walked in. Ask your parents what it felt like the moment you were born. (And if your parents aren't around or if you weren't exactly given the best set of parents, imagine what it's going to feel like when you hold your new baby for the first time) My point is, it doesn't matter what your dream is, because the moment you start seeing it manifest (which is just a fancy word for manifest), you begin to experience a level of connection and joy with God that isn't found very many other places on earth.

All right. I think I've done a good job of taking the long way to define success in this chapter. So, here's the short version. *According to God, success is defined as following Him and pursuing the things He's put in your heart.* Period. There isn't any more or less to that statement. We can rest easy knowing that if we are doing those two things, God considers us successful. And to give that thought some biblical perspective as we close this chapter out, consider the following parable found in Matthew 25, the parable of the talents. If you're not familiar with it, I'll give you the RBRV. (Ricky Borba Revised Version). A man went on a journey and gave three of his employees some money to invest while he was gone. Each employee was not created equal in the "business investment" department, so he gave each one a different amount of money **based on their ability**. The first employee he gave five dollars, the second two dollars and the third he gave a 1993 Susan B. Anthony dollar. The first two employees doubled their money and the third shoved that Susan B. Anthony coin in his junk drawer. When the man returned from his trip, his first two employees showed him their profits, and he was happy. So happy in fact, that he promised both men opportunities to earn more money. Then the third employee stepped into his office. (Let's give this third guy a name. How about…Anakin? Sound good? No idea where I came up with that name, but let's go with it.) So Anakin walks into the office and tells his friend/boss (let's give this guy a name too. How about….Obi-Wan? Again, no idea where I came up with that, but it sounds right), "Obi-Wan, I took your silver dollar here and I shoved it in my junk drawer. Here. You can have it back." At this, Obi-Wan becomes incensed and says "You were the Chosen One! You were supposed to invest my dollar, not bury it! You were supposed to bring balance to the bank account, not leave it in darkness!" Anakin, embarrassed, says the only thing he can think of, which is, "I HATE YOU!" Obi-Wan then tells Anakin that he's lazy and wicked, then takes his silver dollar and gives it to the one of the other guys who invested their money. Obi-Wan wraps his lecture up by telling Anakin that we are all going to be held accountable based on the things we are given in life. What's of note is that the Bible doesn't say that God loves or appreciates those who have more anymore than those who have less. What God does show us is that He **expects us to do something with the talents He's given us.** I'd go as far as to say God needs you to do something with it, because the beauty of what God has given us isn't just for our benefit. In pursuing your dreams and using your talents, you become a blessing and encouragement to others.

As we close this chapter, here's another exercise. At the end of chapter 2, you wrote down a bunch of talents and abilities the Lord has given you. Now, as you've read a little further in this book, I want you to write down some ways you can start using those talents and abilities **today.** Yes, today. And for those of you using your abilities and talents already, there is always room for growth. So take a few minutes here and fill this out.

I've been given talents and abilities that are unique to me. These talents excite me, and I want to start using them more, so here are some practical ways I can either start using them, or start developing them further.......

CHAPTER 5

How to Properly Deal with the Hardships/Rejection That Come With Following Your Dreams

Song to accompany this chapter:
Heaven **by Live**

In the words of the immortal Rocky Balboa, I'd like to start this chapter off with one of the best lines from all 63 Rocky and Creed movies: "The world is a very mean and nasty place and I don't care how tough you are, it will beat you to your knees and keep you there permanently if you let it. You, me, or nobody is gonna hit as hard as life. But it ain't about how hard you hit. It's about how hard you can get hit and keep moving forward." If you haven't ever seen *Rocky Balboa*, it's a great film. And that speech alone is worth the watch. Rocky is telling his son what I'm aiming to do in this chapter, which is to let you know that life is going to hit you, **hard.** Genesis 50:20 NLT (one of my favorite verses to live by, for the record) says "You (the devil) intended to harm me, but God intended it all for good." Or, in the RBRV, "When #$%& hits the fan, God still has a plan."

Whether you're chasing after your dreams or not, life is going to deal you some uppercuts. (I promise I'll tone down the boxing references from here on in.) No one is immune to it. The Bible says it will rain on the just and the unjust. Scholars estimate that 105 billion people have been born since the dawn of time. And since this isn't a book arguing science and the Bible, let's just take that number at face value right now. If I did my math right, one-hundred percent of 105 billion people means that 105 BILLION PEOPLE have had to deal with some sort of adversity in their lives. Adversity doesn't care what age you are, either. Unfortunately, some of us are born with adversity, while some of us don't experience it until a later age. Make no mistake, the hard things in life are coming for you, and there is nothing you can do to stop them. But it's when you add a dream-chaser to the equation that things start to really get "fun." Did you think life was hard before you started chasing your dreams? Just wait until everyone finds out you're done climbing the corporate ladder and want to open a hot dog stand! FEAR NOT, my fellow reader. (Actually, you're not my fellow reader, because I'm writing and you're reading. Sounded good, though.) There ARE things you can learn and begin doing TODAY that can help you deal with the hardships and rejection that come with chasing your dreams.

Years ago, I heard a quote attributed to Elie Wiesel, a man who survived the Holocaust and became a writer, professor, political activist, and Nobel Laureate. The quote I heard attributed to him was in regard to his treatment while in Auschwitz. "The Nazis took my clothes, my food, my family, and my pride away from me. But there was one thing they could never take away from me, no matter how poorly they treated me, and that was my response to them." I'll never forget when I heard that. I was sitting in Bible college listening to the speaker we had brought in for chapel that week, and it floored me. Elie Wiesel was 100% correct. The only thing that no one can **ever** take away from us is our response to things. You are the only one that chooses your reaction to things. Sure, we can say things like "I get so mad when you…" but the reality is, that reaction is still a choice! To take it a step further, think about Jesus as He was getting flogged right before He was put on the cross. What do you make of His response? Do you think He had a right to be angry at the Roman guards inflicting pain on Him? Do you think He would have been well within His rights to respond in any number of different ways than He did? What about when He was put on the cross? At any point did He curse the men who were killing Him? At any point did He call down a legion of angels and annihilate the entire wicked population that was responsible for Him being nailed up there? My point is, despite all the things Jesus was enduring on His final day on earth (before He rose again) He chose to respond well. In fact, He asked God to forgive the ones who were killing Him. Just thinking about that while writing this right now gets me emotional! I have mind-murdered people in my life for **FAR** less! Yet I just gave you examples of two men who chose to respond well during their most difficult hours!

If we were in class and discussing this chapter, point number one to the question of "How do you overcome the hard things that go along with chasing your dreams?" would be: Respond well. You see, if we believe we are made in the image of God, then it is possible for us to do the very things that Jesus Himself did. If Jesus can respond well during His trials, then I can respond well during mine. Once again, the response you give to the difficulties in your life is your decision alone. There isn't anyone who can force you to smile, frown, or anything else. Just to be clear, I am not saying it's never appropriate to be angry or upset or disappointed. Again, I look to Jesus as the example; He certainly wasn't "thrilled" when He walked into that temple and saw what those "religious" folk had done to it. There are times for that righteous anger; there are times to mourn and be sad. The types of responses I'm talking about here are when things aren't going your way, when someone says or does something to you that is legitimately unfair, etc. There's a difference between getting home from vacation and seeing your house has been robbed, which results in anger, fear, and worry, and cussing out the person at Best Buy who refused to let you return the DVD you purchased and tried returning without a receipt. (Oddly specific example, don't you think? I wonder who I'm talking about.)

Responding well isn't something that happens overnight. It's like praying for patience. The more you need to learn to respond well, the more not awesome things will seem to happen in your life. I wish I could say that even now as I write this book that I've mastered it. But I haven't. Something happened to me a couple of months ago that resulted in me getting a big "F" on my report card in the "response" department. The problem was (as is usually the case), I chose to take offense to what was being said and done to me. Proverbs 19:11 says there is joy to be had in overlooking an offense. (By the way, I feel like that should be something you have to agree to when signing up for a social media account. Question 1: "Do you agree to the 23-page terms and services document that you didn't read?" Question 2: "Do you agree to overlook someone's words when they comment on something you posted that you don't agree with?") I have to admit, though, that when I did decide to put on my big-boy pants and stop being "hurt" by what this person said to me and did to me, it was like my soul took a warm bubble bath. Immediately after praying to forgive that person (even though they hadn't asked for forgiveness) I was left feeling closer to God and happier about things in my life. Choosing to be offended corrodes your mental and spiritual life. What's worse is that 10 times out of 10, the person who offended you isn't even thinking about it! You're letting them live rent-free in your head, and that's never good.

When you choose to follow your dreams, everyone seems to have an opinion on why you shouldn't, or why it won't work, or why their plan for your life is better. Believe me, you're going to hear a lot of it when you make it public that you're chasing your dreams. The great thing is that if you can start now learning to respond well to things and not be offended, you'll be way ahead of the game! Instead of responding poorly, which can render you useless for days and months at a time, you'll be able to take those words and actions in stride and use them as ammo to keep going. As my pastor always says, "Every irritation is an invitation to rise to the next level." I believe that statement whole-heartedly.

Point number two is keeping in mind that you are the project. For me, this is an easy comparison to what I'm trying to accomplish because films are typically called projects. So my pastor (you really should meet him, GREAT guy) told me that no matter what film I'm ever a part of, that I am the project. Meaning, God is working in my life to make me more like Him, and less like myself. (John 3:30) His practical and specific exhortation to me was that this path I'm on is going to be full of ups and downs, especially considering that I'm working in the film industry which is notorious for getting your ego bruised. His advice was that if I can refrain from getting too enamored with my highs, and too discouraged by my lows, I would be able to keep a level head and navigate this roller coaster with ease. So far, I'd give myself a B-. There have definitely been some wonderful highs, and conversely, brutal lows. Thanks to his advice and my own ability to remember that I'm the project, I've been able to stay afloat.

When you humble yourself and stop making yourself the author of your own screenplay, it allows you to be teachable and trainable. But when you walk around trying to be the author and perfector of your life, you aren't much good to anyone, let alone yourself. I find that when I'm trying to "drive," as Christians like to say, I always end up in a lane God never intended me to be in. I also find that I get offended easily, angered easily, and generally become someone I wouldn't want one of my daughters dating. Let me be frank here, though; humbling yourself is a **very difficult** thing to do. It often means that even if you're in the right, you agree to see the other person's point of view. You may even end up apologizing for something that one hundred percent was not an offense or wrong, but you apologize anyway, just to smooth the waters. And look, I'm Portuguese and Spanish, so I know full well about having that short fuse fire raging in my belly. If I let myself, I could very easily be the kind of guy that throws dishes, punches walls, gets physical with people, and so on. But thanks to the grace of God, I've by and large been able to keep that kind of disposition out of my life. Which, let me tell you, if you knew my family, you'd agree was a minor miracle, knowing how bad-tempered the men have been throughout our family history.

On any project you work on, there is always a beginning, middle, and end. As such, we as humans fall into the same categories. So, as long as we aren't on our deathbeds about to take our final breath, we're either at the beginning or in the middle of our project. This means that there is room for growth, improvement, recalibration, and maybe even having to start all over to get it right. The point is, when we consider ourselves the project and God the builder, as long as we are willing to be molded, we literally cannot be built incorrectly! God is not a god of chaos and disorder. He is a God of perfection and grace. No matter what your dream is, remember that **you** are the project that God is working on the entire time. For me, any film I work on is eventually going to be collecting dust on a shelf somewhere. The business you own someday will either run its course and close down when you retire, or you'll end up handing it off to someone else when you're done with it. It too has a shelf life. But as long as there is breath in our lungs, we do not have a shelf life!

The final point I want to make is that dealing with rejection and hardships are probably the hardest things to accomplish. The reason it's so hard is that it involves other people. My first two points can be accomplished on your own (with the help of God and counsel), but this final point is something that is going to take a strong will and dedication. One of the most significant sources of your outlook on life and your own self is in regards to who you allow to speak into your life and who you're spending most of your time with. The greatest example of this plays out in the book of Job. Job had the worst advice-giving friends in the history of the world. Their advice was so bad that God literally condemned them. God's "anger burned against them." Seriously! With all the bad advice I've ever been given, I can't say that God spoke to any of those people and condemned them and told them to offer a sacrifice to atone for their idiocrasy.

Back to the point, sorry. Job was going through some legitimately difficult times. Unfortunately, he enlisted the advice of his closest friends. Can you imagine the story of Job had his friends given him wise counsel? The book of Job would have only had about five chapters instead of 42. Wise counsel would have saved Job and his friends from a lot of heartaches.

    The same goes for us, especially when it comes to making a decision like chasing your dreams. Because let me tell you, **people who have given up on their own dreams are going to be the first ones to tell you to quit on yours**. I do want to make something clear right now, though. People won't say that to you because they're being inconsiderate or rude or mean. The reason they'll say this to you is most likely because they have your best interests in mind. Huh? That sounds like a good thing, Ricky. Yes. I know. It *sounds* good. But there's a gigantic difference from your best interests and your **destiny**. Most of the people who love you, if not all, want what's "best" for you. Meaning the type of job or career that affords you the house, car, two weeks of vacation, etc. That's the "dream," right?! Wrong. Hopefully, by this point in the book, you're starting to get a clearer picture of what a true "dream" is, but I digress. It took quite a while for me, but a few years ago I finally found a couple of friends who had my destiny in mind when they gave me advice and encouraged me. Let me break down what these kinds of friendships look like, and what that kind of advice from them sounds like.

Friends and family who have your destiny in mind are the ones who are going to help pick you yourself up off the ground when you're feeling defeated. They're the ones that would be willing to give you the shirt off their back, as opposed to telling you that if you had a "real job" you wouldn't be in this position in the first place. They're the ones who when there is more month than money, they'll swing by with groceries and expect nothing in return. They're the ones that will call you on an idle Tuesday just to tell you that they love you and are encouraged by you. I can go on and on, but you get my point. The types of people you need to make sure you have in your life are the types of people who love you, believe in you and most of all, support you. I've been fortunate to have a wife who (once she came around) has been one of my biggest supporters. I was also fortunate to have had a mother who knew the difference between her son's best interests and his God-given dream. As I mentioned earlier, my mother passed away from cancer, but often times it is her words that ring through my head when things are tough. Sometimes it's not even her words. Sometimes I think about a look she gave me or an unexpected gift that arrived. See the thing is, parents have an incredible effect on the lives of their children! Not just during the years before we move out, but even as married adults, our parents hold life and death in their hands in how they interact with us. I honestly don't know if I'd be writing this book if my mother hadn't believed in me. She was the one who told me above all the other talents she saw me have, that writing was the one she thought I was best at. (I BBQ chicken like NO ONE'S BUSINESS, so I'm not sure she was right...) But the point is that my mom believed in me and encouraged me and told me to keep going. So, I will say this. If you're a parent and you're reading this book, and you think you aren't exactly supporting your child's dreams in the best way possible, put this book down right now and go make it right! (Please come back and finish the book, though, there's a lot of great things ahead. I promise.) Watch as your child's eyes open up and look at you like they never have before. Just go in there right now and say "Hey! I love you and I want you to know that your dream of becoming a _____ is REALLY cool! And I'll do everything I can to help you achieve it, even if I have to learn about it myself!" Talk about changing the course of someone's trajectory. Man, I'm telling you, if more parents were excited like that, this world would be a better place!

Finally (see what I did there? Total pastor move. In the last paragraph I said, "my final point." Then I started this paragraph off with "Finally..."), if you have no earthly idea of how or where to find the type of "destiny in mind" friends, I have a suggestion. Go to places and events where like-minded people will be. I don't mean like-minded as in dream chasers. I mean, if your dream is to become a singer, start hanging around and attending singing competitions. Join a social media group that is focused on your passion. Go online and see if there are any meet-ups in your area of people with similar dreams. There's a huge difference between spending time researching your dream (reading books, taking classes, online research, etc.) and having friendships where you physically spend time with other people who are passionate like you are. It's like adding sugar to the Kool-Aid. Sure, the packet of flavoring tastes edible when you pour it in the water, but once you add sugar, look out! THAT'S when things go from good to GREAT. The same thing happens when you spend time with people who love what you love. Even if your dream isn't a creative or artistic-heavy dream, you can still benefit from spending time with people who are involved in your passion. For example, I'm not at all medically-minded, but my wife is. Her career mandates that twice a year she spend a weekend with other people in the same career, for the purpose of renewing their licenses. And I'm telling you when my wife gets home from those weekend seminars, she's rejuvenated. She's heard and seen things over the course of the weekend that she hadn't thought of before. Other times, she's able to give someone perspective or advice that encourages them, which in turn encourages my wife.

I'm looking down at my word-count and I feel like we are at the halfway point of this book. So, I'd like to ask you to do something, if you're up for it. I want to hear from you. I want to know if what you've read so far has had any impact on you. So, shoot me an email at *borbafett@gmail.com*. Or, let's get crazy and put my phone number out there, you say? Fine! Shoot me a text at **(615) 965-4010**. Seriously text me. Email me. And I will do my best to get back to you. It's important to know someone out there (even if it's just me for now) who supports you. So drop me a quick line and let me know what you think of the book so far, and what your dream is. I'd love to hear from you.

CHAPTER 6

Myth-Breaking[2]

Song for this chapter:
The Crystal Method – *Keep Hope Alive*

Let's face it, more times than not, the only person stopping you from chasing our dreams is you. (I said YOU, in case that wasn't clear.) Admittedly, there are often a lot of obstacles to hurdle when it comes to making your dream a reality, but usually, the biggest obstacle is the battle you wage in your mind. Make no mistake: there is a reason that of the 12 disciples, Jesus had three that he considered close friends. I believe with all my heart that the reason for this was so that in those weak moments, those moments of "Am I sure I'm cut out for this?", Jesus leaned on His three closest friends for encouragement and support. When I think about my own journey, I know that at times the only reason I'm still pursuing and chasing after my dream is because some-

---

[2] Apparently there's some sort of copyright on using the word myth, followed by the word busting. We're looking into it

one in my life gave me a word of encouragement, or was just a sounding board for me to vent my frustrations to. I know beyond a shadow of a doubt that if I were left to my own thoughts and determination, I would have packed it in long ago.

I've never liked it when someone dismisses a **valid** reason for not wanting to do something as an "excuse." I think the word "excuse" not only gets used far too often, but it's used as a blanket word to define any sort of thought or action that is in direct opposition to a said task. Whenever I hear someone use that word in a conversation, my ears perk up and I can start feeling the little fire inside me getting lit. Some people have very valid reasons for not wanting to do something. So in my journey, it's not as easy as dismissing those reasons as "excuses." Sure, sometimes you run into the occasional person that truly does have an excuse for everything, but more often than not, the reason or reasons someone gives for not wanting to do something are at the very least, very real and valid to that person. Now, that doesn't mean just because it's valid to them that their reason is a genuine valid concern in the true sense of the word. Take my aunt, for example. Petrified to fly. Why? You guessed it, the plane might crash. (Ironically, I'm writing this chapter while flying to Virginia from California. Let's hope this isn't the last sentence I ever write.......) At 50 years old, she has only ever flown out of absolute necessity. No amount of reasoning or presentation on the safety of flying compared to driving can dissuade her. Believe me, we've tried. It's just not going to happen. But it would be foolish of me to tell her that her reasoning for not wanting to fly is an "excuse." Not only that, but it would probably hurt her feelings if I were to be so dismissive of her genuine fear.

A flight across the country is six hours. From start to finish, the total time of fear and anxiety related to flying is about a third of a day if you include the drive to the airport and getting on the plane. Now take that fear and anxiety, mix it with following your dreams, and then add in the uncertainty of finances, a clear path to the end goal of your dream, and potentially alienating friends and family because of your choice to go against the grain. This is why the word "excuse" doesn't work at all. There are very valid reasons for not choosing to go after your dreams. And for the record, these types of reasons not to go after the desires of your heart and calling from God go back as far as humankind. Don't believe me? Take a look at these examples of biblical figures who had their own reasons for not wanting to do what God asked them to and put on their heart.

Noah was a drunk. Abraham was too old. Isaac was a daydreamer. Jacob was a liar. Leah was ugly. Joseph was abused. Moses had a stuttering problem. Gideon was afraid. Samson had long hair and was a womanizer.

Rahab was a prostitute. Jeremiah was too young. David was an adulterer (not to mention a murderer). Elijah was suicidal. Isaiah preached naked. Jonah ran from God. Naomi was a widow. Job went bankrupt. John the Baptist ate bugs. Andrew lived in the shadow of his big brother. Peter denied Christ. All the disciples fell asleep while praying (and ran away when Jesus really needed them). Martha worried about everything. The Samaritan woman was divorced (more than once). Mary Magdalene was demon-possessed. Zacchaeus was too small. Timothy had an ulcer. Paul was a Christian-killer. Oh… and Lazarus was dead.

I get it. Some of those examples seem like character flaws and don't fall into the category of "personal reasons not to obey God's calling." However, most of those people verbalized their shortcomings with God, and God used them anyway. Now re-read those examples with an additional phrase added to each sentence.

Noah was a drunk. **God used him.** Abraham was too old. **God used him.** Isaac was a daydreamer. **God used him.** Jacob was a liar. **God used him.** Leah was ugly. **God used her.** Joseph was abused. **God used him.** Moses had a stuttering problem. **God used him.** Gideon was afraid. **God used him.** Samson had long hair and was a womanizer. **God used him.** Rahab was a prostitute. **God used her.** Jeremiah was too young. **God used him.** David was an adulterer (not to mention a murderer). **God used** him. Elijah was suicidal. **God used him.** Isaiah preached naked. **God used him.** Jonah ran from God. **God used him.** Naomi was a widow. **God used her.** Job went bankrupt. **God used him.** John the Baptist ate bugs. **God used him.** Andrew lived in the shadow of his big brother. **God used him.** Peter denied Christ. **God used him.** All the disciples fell asleep while praying (and ran away when Jesus really needed them.) **God used them.** Martha worried about everything. **God used her.** The Samaritan woman was divorced (more than once). **God used her.** Mary Magdalene was demon-possessed. **God used her.** Zacchaeus was too small. **God used him.** Timothy had an ulcer. **God used him.** Paul was a Christian-killer. **God used him.** And finally, Lazarus was dead. **God used him.**

Do you see the pattern here? It doesn't matter what the reason is, whether it's our own self-doubt or if it's something that seems beyond our control. If God has called you to do something, He WILL provide a way for that to be done! God isn't a god who teases or sets us up for failure. If you have a stirring desire in your heart to go after something, then frankly, my friend, you have no business doing anything else with your life! God NEEDS and WANTS you to go after that dream! If reading those biblical examples of men and women being used by God for GREAT things doesn't inspire you, then stop reading right now and find your nearest pharmacy and ask them for some adrenaline. Because when I read those examples, I can't help but think that I'm MORE than capable of achieving the dreams God has in store for me. Faith without works is dead. When you read your Bible or any book about someone who has accomplished something significant in their life, you won't ever see or hear the following statement: "I was sitting on my couch when all of a sudden someone knocked on my door and handed me my opportunity." It doesn't work like that. Just because God gives you a vision for your life does not mean it will automatically come true. A long time ago I learned that the dreams the Lord gives us are of what may come true, contingent on us getting up and putting in some of the effort ourselves. Oh, and while we're in the chapter about debunking myths, here's a really common one. The Bible does not say, "God helps those who help themselves."(Algernon Sydney and Ben Franklin share the "honor" for coining that phrase.) I hear that phrase thrown out a lot. Unfortunately, it's mostly used as a hand slap to someone. When someone is struggling to get by, when things seem bleak, the LAST thing someone should ever say to anyone in that situation is "God helps those who help themselves." What that person is really saying is that it must be due to lack of effort on your part as to why God hasn't come through yet. As if God has some tally sheet that He's marking, and as soon as you get enough in the plus column, He'll open the floodgates. Wrong. God is ALWAYS working on your behalf, so if your dreams aren't realized yet, it isn't because God is smiting you. Speaking from personal example, God doesn't just hand over the keys to the Ferrari the minute you get it in your head you want one. He takes us on a journey of not only self-discovery so we can find out what we're made of, but also a journey of finding out who HE is and what HE is made of!

On this journey of becoming a filmmaker, I've experienced some incredible highs and very low valleys. But through it all, the most important thing I've gained is a deeper relationship with God. I go back to that verse in Matthew that has become sort of my life verse. Matthew 6:26-27 NIV. "Look at the birds of the air; they do not sow or reap or store away in barns, and yet your heavenly Father feeds them. Are you not much more valuable than they? Can any one of you by worrying add a single hour to your life?" Every single time without fail, God has provided for me, despite my self-doubt, myths about why I can't accomplish my dreams, poor choices, and in some cases flat out sin or disobedience. He's a loving Father though, and He doesn't see time linearly. Part of why I think we get so down on ourselves is that when we screw up, we live in that moment. Sometimes for hours, sometimes for days and weeks, sometimes for months and years. As humans, we're incapable of seeing our future, so we are forced to deal with things in real time. God, on the other hand, has the luxury of seeing our entire life at once. Think of it like this. To us, our lives are like a ruler. We start at the left side and work our way inch by inch to the end of the ruler. Along that ruler are milestones, both good and bad. Now, imagine we take that ruler and chop it up into a thousand pieces, each representing one of those good or bad milestones. Then put them in a bowl, shake them up and dump them on the floor. Now you're beginning to understand how God sees our lives. He looks from above and sees our greatest moments and biggest failures all at the same time. This gives Him the distinct privilege of not being stuck on a moment in time. Now, with that in mind, are you ready for the REAL mind-blower? When you ask God for forgiveness, along with accepting His son as your personal savior, all those moments of sin and failure disappear. The Bible says God chooses to forget our sin when we ask Him to!

Imagine the ability to have no clue about all your mistakes and failures, only knowing your accomplishments and positive moments in life. It would change the way you talk, act, and go about life. Well, actually maybe being aware of only how awesome we are would result in a world full of sociopaths. So, why don't we do this instead; why don't we try walking, talking, and acting like we are fully aware that God sees us in the way I described a paragraph ago, as His beautiful, talented, and perfect children. Because in doing that, it gives us the motivation and mindset to never give up going after our dreams. Remember, what you think about God is the most important thing about you. So if you can get that part of your life nailed down, imagine the possibilities.

Something I heard a friend tell me a while back, when he was trying to open his own car detailing business and kept running into problem after problem, was "If it was easy, everyone would be doing it."

CHAPTER 7

The World Needs You to Follow Your Dreams Because YOU Are the Only One Who Can Do It Your Way!

Song for this chapter:
Frank Sinatra — *My Way*

In the movie *Full Metal Jacket,* one of the characters says the following phrase, which I didn't realize was a full-on creed until I looked it up about two minutes ago. "This is my rifle. There are many like it, but this one is mine." There's a lot more to that creed, but the crux is that while there might be a lot of similar rifles, there is only one that is uniquely yours. Now, do me a favor and substitute the word "dream" instead of "rifle," and you'll start to see how important your dreams should be to you.

My dream, being a film director/producer/actor is a dream that many people have had and accomplished in the history of the world. Think of all the great films you've seen in your life. Think about all the bad ones too, if you want. In all those films, though, do you know what's unique about them? The director of that film brought their own unique vision to the process of creating that film. Had another director stepped in, you would not have the same film, even though the script would have been the exact same one, word for word.

Your dream, whatever it is, might be a dream that is extremely unique in that little to no others have ever done it. It might be a dream that thousands or millions of people have accomplished before you and will after you. But there's one thing about your dream that no one else on earth can ever claim about it, and that is that however you choose to perform the tasks surrounding it, no one else is capable of doing it the way you are. No one will sing like you. No one is going to be a foster parent like you. No one will fabricate sheet metal the way you will. No one will sell hot dogs (apparently I really need to consider this as an alternative to my dream of being a filmmaker, as this is the third time I've mentioned it) the way you do. On and on, etc., etc. You are the only person qualified to do it "your way." (Dear Burger King attorneys, I said "do it your way," not "have it your way.")

Imagine it is the year 1899. You're at home, thinking up some sort of widget that you just know in your soul could be special if only you could wrap your mind around it 100%. Now, imagine you take it to your buddy, a Mr. Charles Duell, for his opinion on it. Now finally, imagine he gives you the response he is famously quoted as having said: Charles H. Duell was the Commissioner of US patent office in 1899. Mr. Duell's most famous attributed utterance is that "everything that can be invented has been invented." Apparently, Mr. Duell hadn't read this book, because if he had, he would have known that every person on earth has the ability to create something the world has never seen.

Admittedly, there are quite a few truly unique inventions and vocations, things that cannot be duplicated. But in doing some quick memory jogging, I'm more inclined to believe that some of the world's most impressive inventions and vocations have been born from things already in existence. For example, what if Steve Jobs had decided that the computers and phones in circulation at the time were "good enough." We'd be without smartphones and personal computers. What if the Wright brothers decided that ground transportation at twenty miles per hour sufficed. We'd be without airplanes. On the vocation side of things, what if William and Catharine Booth decided that the world had enough ways to bring salvation to the poor, destitute, and hungry by meeting both their "physical and spiritual needs." We wouldn't have the Salvation Army.

It's always fascinated me, and I do mean fascinated in every sense of the word, when I've met someone or come to know someone, and found out their dreams are 180 degrees different than mine. Sometimes I have to catch myself from saying something like "Seriously?" or, "Come on, really?" Being a filmmaker is the only "job" I've ever wanted. I can't imagine doing anything else. I think about it, I dream about it, I study it, etc. etc. It's not something I do. It's a part of who I am. So, when I meet someone who tells me that their dream job is to build houses or become a CPA, my mind goes haywire for a second. Sometimes I want to shake them and ask, "DO YOU EVEN KNOW WHAT YOU'RE MISSING OUT ON?!" But that's just it! They probably want to shake ME and ask me the same thing. It's a beautiful thing, the way God wired us. Just taking my own children as an example, five kids and (most likely, because two can barely talk as of this writing) five different personalities and career choices. All my kids came from the same two people (trust me, I've done the DNA tests and watched the hospital security footage over and over) and all of my kids are vastly different in who they are and what they want their lives to be like when they grow up. It makes sense. We're God's children, so the fact that six billion of us all want something different out of life just goes to show that God delights in our differences. Because if He didn't delight in them, we'd ALL be CPA's.

Confession. I don't read a lot of books. I actually don't love reading, to be totally honest. So, every book I have read, I do the same thing. And that is, I thumb through each chapter to see which chapter is the shortest, so I can look forward to it. This is that chapter. Short and sweet. Kind of reminds me of a funny birthday song we used to sing at the Olive Garden when I worked there. If the waiters and waitresses (It's okay to call them that still, right?) were burnt out from singing, instead of singing the official Olive Garden birthday song (which I still remember to this day), we would sing the following: "Thissssssssssssss is your birthday song! It isn't very long!"

CHAPTER 8

Your Dreams and Visions From God Are What *May* Come True. Not of What *Will* Come True[3]

Song for this chapter:
Johnny Cash – *Rusty Cage*

Acts 2:17 CEV says, ""When the last days come, I will give my Spirit to everyone. Your sons and daughters will prophesy. Your young men will see visions, and your old men will have dreams." Now, I don't know how close we are to the "last days," but I do know a lot of men and women who have had dreams and visions. And truth be told, I don't run in very "religious" circles. I have a tight-knit core of Christian friends and a Christian father-

---

[3] Don't worry, there's an easy fix to make them come true.

figure/mentor in my life, but I don't work at a church, I don't attend a ton of Christian concerts or events, and I certainly don't profess to experience the prophetic gifts often, if at all. But I myself have had three very vivid dreams that were from the Lord, and in my circle of Christian friends, almost all of them have had dreams or visions at some point. Not that I'm a biblical scholar, but I think the reason God chooses to give us these dreams and visions is that dreams happen 100% of the time when we are sleeping, which is when our minds are finally at rest. I've also found that visions tend to happen when someone is either tired or deep in prayer. There's something about quieting our minds that allows God's voice to be heard and seen more clearly. The most prophetic vision/dream I've had in my life occurred on a night where I was **extremely** frustrated with God. I went to bed angry, on top of being mentally, emotionally, spiritually, and physically exhausted. (I think I covered all the LY's there.)

When God chooses to speak to us, it's significant. Think about the stories you remember most from the Bible. Most likely, they're stories like when God spoke to Moses, Abraham, David, and others. There's something special about hearing from our father, whether it's the lowercase f type, or the capital F Father in heaven. As a father of five, I've learned that my kids are most attentive and receptive when I get down to their level and speak to them eye to eye. When we're sleeping, our eyes are closed, which is how they are when we pray. In a sense, God is coming down to our level when He gives us dreams and visions.

The most significant thing I heard regarding our dreams and visions from God, is the title of this chapter. *Your dreams and visions from God are of what may come true. Not of what will come true.* What does that mean? Well, simply put, I believe it means you can't just sit around and expect your dreams to come true without putting any effort into them. I know, I'm Captain Obvious, right? But here's the thing. How many talented people do you know who also have "big dreams" for those talents, but do next to nothing with them? I can think of quite a few in my life off the top of my head. And to be honest, it drives me crazy. I want to grab them by the shoulders and shake them like one of those 1950's exercise belts that were supposed to melt stomach fat away. (Those were a thing! Really! https://www.youtube.com/watch?v=1lCnG9hWC6w) Other than being awesome at being "Ricky Borba," I've never really possessed the kind of body, skills, or anything else that would set me apart from the rest of the crowd. But I've met a lot of people who were incredibly blessed in sports, music, acting, or otherwise. So, like the movie *Rudy*, I always wonder what my determination and refusal to quit would look like if I had the skillsets that some of my friends and family have. I always thought if I were a couple of inches taller, I could have been the high school quarterback. Well, a couple of inches taller and about 25 more pounds of muscle. I always told myself I could throw a football over them mountains... Yeah... Coach woulda put me in the fourth quarter, we would've been state champions. No doubt. No doubt in my mind.

That's why a very long time ago in my life, I made the decision that I was going to outdream, outwork, and outfrustrate everyone else in my life. Since I didn't have the physical or socio-economic advantages that others in my life seemed to have, my heart (in the intestinal fortitude sense) had to rise way above the average dream-chaser. Earlier in the book, I mentioned that the only thing preventing you from achieving your dreams is you. I live by that. So, I was **not** going to be my own worst enemy by allowing myself to be the reason I didn't make it. Not by a lack of effort, anyway.

The other side of the "making your dreams happen" coin is called comfort. Let's face it, life is hard, and the one thing that can make life a little easier is not just steady income, but a **lot** of steady income. You'll never meet a group of people harder to convince to follow their dreams than those who make a lot of money in their careers. I can't blame them, either! I'll tell you right now, had I begun making hundreds of thousands of dollars in any one of the 23 jobs I had before I started pursuing my dreams, I guarantee that you would not be reading this book right now. The accumulation of wealth would have not only prevented me from pursuing my dreams, but it would have also prevented me from growing deeper with the Lord. Now, let me just say this before you toss this book in the trash because you think I'm knocking wealth. I'm **not**. I want to make a **ton** of money-making films and following my dreams. I'm saying for ME, had I, Ricky Borba, made a lot of money before I became a filmmaker, I would have **absolutely** called it a day and packed it in. I would have bought the house, the yacht, the flat black Cadillac Escalade and taken more vacation days than workdays. I know myself. Wealth early on would have caused the pursuit of my calling and dreams to come to a screeching halt.

I called that coin "comfort" for a reason. Because from person to person, comfort is defined differently. My comfort coin would have been wealth early on. Your comfort coin is going to be unique to you. But whatever it is, if you allow it to, it will push your dreams off for a long time, maybe even permanently. I don't think it was easy for the 12 disciples to give up their careers. Sure, in the Bible it's a matter of two sentences that separate "Hey, drop those fishing nets and follow me" to them actually doing so. But I imagine there was some deep soul-searching going on. Maybe it took minutes, maybe less, but I guarantee you, each one of those men thought about what life would be like when they left what was comfortable. But as is the case for you, following their calling began with that very first step of obedience. The minute you say, "Okay, I'm doing this!" and take that first step, the next steps are always into uncertainty. How many steps are you willing to take is the question.

No one was going to show up on my doorstep saying, "Ricky, I want you to direct a film I will finance. Your time is now" after I had my dreams and visions from the Lord to become a filmmaker. I had to be proactive about it. I couldn't sit and play Fallout 4, hoping a check would come in the mail for $750,000 with the subject line of "Go make your movie!" And that's what I mean by your dreams and visions from the Lord are of what can happen, not what will happen. Abraham wouldn't have been given everything the Lord promised him had he not obeyed and put the dream into motion. I wouldn't have directed The Talking Tree and My Brothers' Crossing had I not gone out and done what was necessary to put myself in a position to meet producers and investors. If you want your dreams to come true, **you cannot be passive about it**. The beautiful thing about being proactive and working hard toward your dreams is that you will undoubtedly find that God will open doors and pave the way for you to achieve those dreams. I could write a whole other book on the incredible favor I've had over the last eight years when it's come to divine meetings, relationships, and appointments. If you're constantly reminding yourself that God is in control of everything, then you can relax and be expectant for Him to blow your mind by creating scenarios, situations and circumstances that make no earthly sense that propel you toward reaching the finish line.

God isn't a God who teases. He's not going to put a desire in your heart, only to get you inches away from it before pulling it away forever. The easy fix to making your dreams come true is when you continue to believe in Him, obey His words and put Him first as you go down your path. When you do that, you'll find yourself further along the path than you could have ever imagined. It might not look like how you imagined it, but I guarantee you, you'll admit to yourself that it's better than anything you could have come up with yourself.

CHAPTER 9

In Addition to Following Your Own Dreams and NEVER Giving Up, You're Also Called to Support Other People's Dreams

Song for this chapter:
Incubus - *Dig*

Pop quiz. What's everyone's favorite thing to talk about? Themselves. Ready for another one? Pop quiz, hotshot. There's a bomb on a bus. Once the bus goes 50 miles an hour, the bomb is armed. If it drops below 50, it blows up. What do you do? What do you do? Okay, back to my original pop quiz. It's not just about you.

(Trademark Rick Warren, I believe. Ha.) That's crazy talk, right? *It's not just about you.* While the feeling you get when you talk to someone about your dreams is pretty awesome. On the flip side, the feeling someone else gets when they're talking about their dreams to someone who couldn't care less is demoralizing.

As a film director, I've learned something pretty invaluable. There's a huge difference between an actor who is in character and engrossed in the scene and an actor who is just waiting for the other person to finish their line, so they can say theirs. There's a disingenuous feeling you can pick up on when you notice this happening. It's the same thing when you're talking to someone who is obviously just waiting for you to finish talking so that they can speak. (If you're guilty of this, KNOCK IT OFF.) You know that old saying, "We have two ears and one mouth for a reason." Well, there's a Bible verse that kind of started that whole train of thought, and it's from James. James 1:9 NIV, to be exact: "My dear brothers and sisters, take note of this: Everyone should be quick to listen, slow to speak..."

Why is this important, and how does it fit into supporting someone else, you ask? Great question. I'm glad I'm answering it for you. We live in a world where we are constantly bombarded with negativity. And a lot of that negativity has to do with the fear of failure. That's why it's important to listen to people. Because once you actually invest your mind and heart into what they're sharing with you, you become far more than just a listener. You become an investor. When you take the time to close your phone, put it on silent, and then in your pocket or purse, and give that person your full, undivided attention, you change their world. And once that happens, the sky is the limit in terms of their countenance. You can see their happiness and excitement permeating from every pore on their body. There's nothing like it. It's electric.

Take a minute right now and think of the people in your life. Is there someone in your life right now that you kind of maybe consider "crazy" for going against the grain and pursuing their dreams? Have you maybe kinda sorta at one time or another not been the most supportive to them? Well, if you have that person in mind, why don't you whip your phone out right now and shoot them a text? You can make it short and sweet. Just let them know you admire them for going after their dreams. And if you're feeling extra nice, let them know you're there for them if they need an ear. Go ahead. I'll wait.

Thanks for doing that. Congrats on being a great person. You win 200 points. (Points have no cash value. Points expire when you finish reading this sentence.)

Thinking back on my life, some of my favorite moments have been when I've given someone a chance at something. Whether it be a role in one of my projects, the opportunity to help me with something I could have done myself, or the ultimate honor of carrying my luggage as I've traveled, there is something special about seeing someone achieve something they weren't sure they could even do themselves. That aside, when you invest and believe in people in that way, you've made a friend and ally for life. At some point in every successful person's life, someone had to say "YES" to them at some point. If you have an opportunity to be someone's "Yes man (or woman)", just get crazy with yourself and do it. The worst that could happen is that they're going to fail. And even if that happens, they will still be eternally grateful you believed in them.

And before I close out this chapter, I thought it might be helpful to list ways you can support other people's dreams. Financially. With your time. With your talents. With your words. Tell them the truth. Be a role model for them. (And no, I'm not saying you go up to them and say "Hey, I'm going to be your role model now, okay? Great. Now, look at how awesome I am." I'm talking about leading a life worth imitating.) Share yourself with them. (Don't only show them how cool and put together you are. Let them know your struggles and hangups. Be authentic.) Challenge them. Ask GREAT questions. And finally, most importantly, pray for them. And don't just SAY you're going to pray for them. I've made a habit that if I tell, text or otherwise notify someone that I'll pray for them, as SOON as those words leave my mouth or my fingers, I pray for them right then and there. We have so many distractions in our day that it's hard enough to remember to take the trash out, let alone pray for someone you talked to 6 hours ago. If you say you're going to pray for someone, do it right then and there. Trust me, it's pretty powerful.

CHAPTER 10

Stay Humble in Your Success

Song to accompany this chapter:
Johnny Cash – *I Walk the Line*

"Vanity. Definitely my favorite sin." That's the last line of one of the coolest films of the '90s, *The Devil's Advocate*. (Incredible performance by Al Pacino!) Al Pacino's character is basically the devil incarnate, and at the end of the movie, we are flipped back to the opening scene of the film, with the main character having seen how his choices would lay out his future. Bottom line, his choices were not good ones, and they lead to a lot of death and destruction. So now, armed with that knowledge, he has an opportunity to make a different choice where it all started. And guess what? He doesn't. He makes the same decision. I for one would like to think if I could see what my choices today resulted in down the road, I would make wise ones, but who am I kidding?

I'd most likely make the same prideful, sinful, arrogant decisions with future knowledge.

And I don't know about you, but the majority of my bad decisions come from one place: pride. Let's pretend this is a high school speech by the valedictorian right now. Ready? Webster's dictionary defines pride as a feeling or deep pleasure or satisfaction derived from one's own achievements, the achievements of those with whom one is closely associated, or from qualities or possessions that are widely admired." Okay, okay, sooooooo, nothing too wrong there. Pride in and of itself doesn't seem so bad. But what happens when we add "ful" to the end of that word? PrideFUL is defined as having an excessively high opinion of oneself. Ah. There's the problem. Like most things in our lives, left unchecked, an attribute or characteristic God meant for good, and as a reflection of Him, can get perverted and distorted into something ugly. In this case, pride can turn into basically thinking you're God. Well, a God. Not the God. (*Groundhog Day*, anyone?)

I remember stepping out of my car and onto that film set for day 1 of *The Talking Tree*. There were 50 people there. Actors, crew, caterers, family, friends. Fifty might not sound like a lot when you consider some big-budget films have hundreds and hundreds of people, but 50 was a lot. We were in a small prison kitchen, and it felt crowded. As I sat down in my director's chair, I kind of felt like Captain Kirk in his command chair on the USS Enterprise. I had the ship. I set the heading. Everyone there was "under my command" in essence. Thirty-nine years, and it had all come down to this. Was I going to let it all go to my head? Was I going to turn into a tyrant, as I've heard a lot of directors do? I looked around that kitchen set and took a deep breath.

And then I prayed. I thanked God for this opportunity. And then I asked Him to use me and keep me humble. For the next 17 days, we shot that film in three cities, with 12 to 14-hour workdays. It was hard work, long hours, constant putting out of fires, all while balancing egos, personalities, and opinions of everyone on set. This isn't a job for everyone, directing. But it was the job for me. And by the grace of God, it never felt like work, and things never went awry. I'd like to say I treated everyone with respect and class, and (for the vast majority of the time) kept my cool. (There was one night, in particular, I raised my voice and let the crew know I was upset with their continued ignoring of my request, but that was the one and only time I had to do that.) By the end of the shoot, the greatest thing that happened was not the final time I yelled "cut." It wasn't the after-party. It wasn't all the times I was told "good job." No, it was two separate instances where a PA (Production Assistant. Basically, the lowest title you can have on a film set) came to me to tell me how much they appreciated my treatment of them. One of them even said it was the first time in memory that they felt like they were treated like a human with value.

Now, before you roll your eyes and think to yourself, "Okay guy, calm down, don't let that whole pride thing swell up right now," the reason I'm mentioning that is not that I want you to see how "great" I am. I mention it because I've been that PA. I've been yelled at by the director and star before, in front of scores of people. I remember what it was like as I walked away feeling like I was four inches tall. I was able to use those moments of brokenness and shame in my life, to keep myself humble and appreciative of the people working "under" me, and thankfully they noticed it. Also, in full disclosure, just to be transparent and let you know what my first thought was after signing my director's contract and seeing the money hit our account for the film, I wanted to call about four people and rub it in their faces that I had "made it." I'm telling you, those four guys deserved it. They treated me horribly, took advantage of me, and otherwise beat me up mentally and emotionally. I wanted to remind them what they said and did to me, and tell them how awesome I was now, and how I bet they were sorry they hadn't treated me better. So, you see, I am under no illusion that I am pure-hearted. I am the worst of sinners. Moving on…

One of my best friends is a guy who is an entrepreneur. He also happens to be an aspiring actor. So I gave him an opportunity to audition for a role in the film, and he crushed it. On the days he wasn't filming, he hung out on set with his wife and prayed over people and kind of became my armor bearer during the shoot. A few months after the dust settled from the film, we had lunch at Roundhouse Deli in Roseville, CA. (They have the best tri-tip tacos on the planet. If you are ANYwhere near the Sacramento area, you have to stop in try them.) As an entrepreneur, he told me he had been working under a guy in his mid 30's for the last year or so, in one of those upstart networking marketing companies. He told me that as soon as that guy got even a little success, his entire attitude changed. He began treating people badly, he started doing underhanded things to earn more money, and, in his words, became a completely different person. My friend said, "I will never work with him again." Then he said, "I'm really proud of you for how you handled yourself on set. You're the same guy off and on the set." So, I asked him what the difference was between myself and the other guy. I'll never forget his answer. "You kept people like me close to you. We wouldn't have let you become a tyrant. You let us in and allowed us to speak into your life. This other guy didn't. He shut everyone else out and became a one-man show."

So, I have to admit something. I didn't have a master plan regarding all of that. I didn't sit down and plan out that I needed to keep my close friends close as I got closer and closer to my dreams. I'm just simply not the type of person to fade away from friendships, so shutting them out wasn't ever going to happen in the first place. I say that because it would have been really cool sounding, and easy, to say, "I learned all of that from Jesus." Jesus does teach these things, but I didn't intentionally keep my friends close because I had Jesus on my mind. However...

Within Jesus' 12 disciples, He had his inner three. John, James, and Peter. He had 12 close guys, but within those 12, he kept three of them even closer than the other nine. For me, the lesson in that is that no matter what you do in life, no matter what you're going through, you absolutely cannot do it alone. You need a couple or a few people who are able to speak truth into your life whether you like hearing it or not. Remember, wounds from a friend can be trusted. (Proverbs 27:6) The only way I was going to remain humble as my calling (a particularly self-gratifying calling if I would allow it) came to fruition was if I allowed my closest trusted friends to keep me humble and honest.

I'm not at all suggesting that Jesus needed those three guys to keep *Himself* humble. What I'm saying is that he did need them as shoulders to cry on from time to time. He needed those three guys to both celebrate the good times with and commiserate with during the bad times. So, if Jesus, the Son of God, needed close friends while on earth, then we probably need 300 close friends. Do yourself a favor and start with one, then work your way up from there.

You need to know something. There are people watching you. People who are looking to you to see how you're going to react when things get awful, and how you're going to react when things go great. These people are not only watching to see how you're going to handle it, but these people are watching because they're trying to decide if it's worth it for them to go after their own dreams. Make no mistake. You are being watched and evaluated. And after they've evaluated you for how you handle the ups and downs of following your dreams, they are going to put the microscope on you for how you handle yourself when your dreams come true. (Which they will. Your dreams, that is. Come true.) They're going to be waiting in line with a baseball bat, ready to smack you upside the head the moment you say or do something self-serving. They were the silent masses during your journey, but they'll become the vocal majority once you mess up or do something out of character. Trust me, as I'm speaking from experience. It's the world we live in with social media. The trick is to not give those types of people anything to talk about. At ALL times, think of yourself as the production assistant. Think of yourself as the intern who is going on a coffee run for the bigwigs at the company. Actually, better yet, let's go biblical on this one. 1 Peter 5:6-7 NIV says: "Humble yourselves, therefore, under God's mighty hand, that he may lift you up in due time. Cast all your anxiety on him because he cares for you." Humble yourselves, so that God, who is higher than any other, can lift you up when you're ready.

CHAPTER 11

My Inspirational Facebook Posts That People Seem to Like

My favorite social media platform is Facebook. Unfortunately, it's my favorite for selfish reasons. While I do enjoy having a birds-eye view of my friends' lives, the reason I enjoy Facebook is that I can write there. Twitter limits me to what feels like three sentences. Instagram is, well, Instagram, and other platforms simply don't have the same structure as Facebook does when it comes to sharing the written word. I've been on Facebook since 2008, and while I've posted my fair share of completely useless stuff on there, there have been a few posts that seem to have resonated with people, within the context of following your dreams. I'm going to paste a few of the most commented and shared posts of mine on the following pages, in the hopes that they will encourage you too.

September 8th, 2015: (I'm putting this one first even though it's chronologically out of order because it is my most commented and shared status of all-time).

My parents split the day my sophomore year of high school started. I was 16. I am the oldest of five. (Just four of us back then.) It was an extremely fast and difficult transition going from having both parents in the same house, living a few yards from MC Hammer in a very affluent Fremont neighborhood, to my parents being apart and moving into a very small home.
I went from barely speaking a need or want into existence and having it met, to almost the opposite. Very quickly too. Both of my mom's siblings and their families were living with us in that three-bedroom house.
I wasn't working just yet. I got my first job a few months after the split if memory serves. So I don't know how I came up with the $3 to buy my own bottle of grape juice, but I remember going to the Albertson's by my house and buying it. I didn't want anyone else in the house to know I had it. It was mine. I wasn't about to share it with anyone. So, I walked into the bedroom I shared with my two brothers and two cousins, opened it up, took a sip and put it under my bed. I followed this routine for two more days after school. But something happened on the third day.
I took a sip of the grape juice on the third day, and it tasted sour. I was confused for a second until I realized

what happened. It had fermented. I remember having a watershed moment right there in my bedroom by myself. My selfishness had caused something good and beneficial to become rotten and unusable.

That was 21 years ago. But to this day I remember that incident often. I've been given an incredible amount of talents, blessings, and gifts (whatever word you want to use). I've been trusted and entrusted with a lot of "grape juice." But if I'm not careful, if I start to think even for a minute that those things are just for me, just to be used for my own gain, not only will they surely rot away, but they won't benefit anyone else either. That grape juice would have been a nice treat for my siblings and cousins if I had decided to share it with them. Sure, it would have all been gone in one sitting, but we would have enjoyed it together.

Are you keeping gifts to yourself? Do you have a talent, ability, gift, or skill that you haven't used for anyone but yourself? Perhaps you have an abundance of finances you can use to help someone with. Maybe you have time to offer. Maybe your own story, words, or art can speak to someone. The point is, we ALL have something we can offer to others around us that can benefit them, even if only for a moment. I promise you, if you're willing to use your gifts and talents for others, you'll not only bless them but become better at those very things you're sharing.

October 30th, 2012

We have an ant problem here at the new house. This morning when I woke up and went into the kitchen, Raelyn's sippy cup with juice had spilled onto the hardwood floor into the kitchen. There must have been 50 ants around the puddle of juice. Most of the ants, however, had drowned inside the sugary pool of juice, as there were only a few who were alive on the border. It got me thinking. What if God gave you everything you wanted in abundance? What if all of a sudden you were given a windfall of cash, responsibility, etc.? The reality is, much like the ants, we would probably "drown" because we wouldn't know how to handle obtaining everything we want in one fell swoop. There's a reason we need to and should work hard to obtain things in life: so that when we have smaller portions of what we desire, we learn at that time to be good stewards with it. There's nothing wrong with wanting more than what we have; the problem arises when, much like the ants, we aren't content with what we already have. Be content with what you have today. Try to go a whole day without yearning for more. Instead, be grateful and content with what you already have, because chances are you'd probably mishandle an abundance of whatever it is you feel like you don't have enough of.

February 6th, 2014

I've been trying a lot harder to get even better at following my dreams and what I believe what God has for me. I've cut my FB and video game time down, I've been listening to more sermons online and reading my Bible more intently.

All that is to say, I'm doing the best I can to press into God and lean on His promises for my life. I'd say that for me, one of the ways God communicates with me from time to time is dreams. Some are literal, some are what's going to be down the road, some I need to really seek understanding on. Unfortunately, Satan also knows that God communicates with us in dreams. Last night I had a very discouraging dream (uh oh, here comes a wacky and crazy person statement) where a demon who was sent by Satan began telling me lies about myself and my future. Without going into detail about the dream, I am 100% positive this was an act of the enemy. But here's the cool thing. I was EXTREMELY defiant towards the demon in my dream, and I SHOUTED that I would NEVER stop pursuing my dreams or trusting in God to run my life. I have no idea how long in real-time the dream lasted, but it felt like an hour or so in my dream. My point in posting this is for a few reasons. First, ANY time you pursue something bigger than yourself, or you begin to chase your dreams no matter the cost, you will ALWAYS face opposition. It might come in the form of

finances, discouragement from family and friends, running into brick wall after brick wall and so on. "If it were easy, everyone would be doing it" is a good phrase to remember. Secondly, the minute I began declaring the name of God in my dream, the demon fled. The Bible says that they tremble at the name of Jesus and that they flee when His name is mentioned. It's encouraging to me when verses from the Bible ring true and happen in my life, word for word. And finally, the dream I had let me know I was on the right track. Not to pat my own back, but it's really encouraging to me to know that the things I am pursuing have the enemy scared. I know God is going to protect my family and me. Satan has no authority here and has no power over Christians. Amen. So to my non-Christian friends and Christian friends who are pursuing their passions and dreams, keep going. Never ever stop. Don't ever let anything make you quit. You could be right around the corner from breakthrough.

November 15th, 2018

Today is the last day of principal photography (filming the movie) for The Talking Tree. We have two more scenes to shoot on December 3rd, but as far as the main cast and crew go, today is it.
I obviously knew this day was coming. I'm not going to lie, it's sad to think about. Kind of like summer

camp coming to an end. So yesterday I took a moment and stood across the street from my best friend Justin's house where we spent all day filming. There were 50+ people hustling and bustling in and around his house, doing their various jobs on set. It was a moment for me. I was full of awe and thankfulness for God keeping His promises, looking at all of those people who would have never have met otherwise. Over the last two and a half weeks of filming, the people working on my film as cast and crew have all begun networking and planning other projects with each other. It was a special feeling for me.

I couldn't help but ask myself, what if you had given up on your dream when things got tough? What if you didn't believe God's plan for you? What if, despite every fiber of your being pushing you toward filmmaking your entire life, you decided to play it safe and get a "real" job? The answer was literally in front of my eyes, The Talking Tree would have never been made, and all those people interacting with each other yesterday would never have met.

The point I took away from all those thoughts was this: that your dreams aren't just about you. The decision to follow your dreams also impacts the lives of those around you. There's something unique and special about being around people who follow their dreams and are passionate about their work. So for me, when God puts a desire in my heart and asks me to pursue something, I *know* if I put in the effort to get there, He will guide me. God *isn't a god who teases. When He promises something, it's a done deal. And although there might be bumps in the road on the journey, He has a 100% track record of fulfilling those promises He's made to you.*

I can't wait to share The Talking Tree with all of you. Quite a few of our very famous and very experienced actors have all said the same thing, that we are making something special here. I believe this film is going to be seen by millions of people and have an impact in their lives. I'll save all my thank yous for another post, but I woke up this morning and wanted to share what I just wrote with all of you.

Have a great Thursday, everyone. Make today count. Keep going after your dreams. Amazing, incredible things are just on the horizon if you do.

January 20th, 2020

This is Kyle Shanahan (a picture accompanied this post), the 49ers head coach, sitting on the floor of the locker room last year after the last game. The 49ers had just gone 4-12, which was a worse record than the year before when he was a first-year coach. Things looked bleak.

But.

He stayed the course, believed in himself and the team around him, and now the 49ers, just one year later, are headed to the Super Bowl. I LOVE this photo because I can relate to it a lot. If you've been my friend on Facebook for longer than five minutes, you know my life-long dream of being a filmmaker came to fruition in the last 14 months. I had many "sitting on the locker room floor after a 4-12 season" moments.

So, I just wanted to take this opportunity to encourage all of you who are pursuing your dreams that it's OKAY to sit on the locker room floor and reflect for a minute when things are down. The key is to GET BACK UP after you've assessed everything and GET BACK IN the fight. Your dreams are attainable! Don't let anyone or anything tell you differently, or stop you. YOU are the only one who can prevent your dreams from coming true. This year will see the release of both the films I've directed in the last 14 months. Who knows, maybe I'll hoist a trophy in front of a national audience as a reward for them, but that's not the goal. The goal is to keep pushing forward through all the obstacles to achieve what you're going after. If I can do it, SO CAN YOU.

December 5th, 2022

On the eve of my birthday, here are things I think I think after 45 years:
1. Whatever amount of pasta you think you've grabbed to make for yourself is wrong.

2. *There is no shame in taking days off and doing nothing during the week once in a while. You do not have to "get after it" every single day. If God chose to rest, so should you.*
3. *It takes less effort to encourage and love on someone than it does to tear someone down or think negatively about them. You read that right. Less effort to encourage and love than it does to be negative.*
4. *9.5 times out of 10, your kids are not intentionally trying to annoy you.*
5. *God's grace goes way further and deeper than any human can understand in a lifetime. Just using examples from my own circle of friends, there is nothing you've done that can separate you from God's love and grace.*
6. *Sometimes there are people who you have to cut out of your life. Still love them, still pray for them, but that doesn't mean they belong having access to you.*
7. *You can never spend enough time with your parents.*
8. *Being content doesn't and shouldn't have anything to do with your socio-economic status.*
9. *Prayer absolutely works, even when the answer is "No" or "Wait."*
10. *School drop off and pick up lines were a result of the fall of man. I'm certain of it.*
11. *Life is way too short to spend two-thirds of it working in a career you aren't passionate about.*
12. *Typically, you don't need as much sleep as you think.*

13. *Golf is not a sport. Fight me.*
14. *People who are concerned about your best interests are good to have; people who are concerned about your destiny are worth their weight in gold.*
15. *I'm not going to stop being a picky eater.*
16. *The absolute most important thing you can give your children is your quality time.*
17. *The feeling of achieving your dreams is something that can't be described.*
18. *Listening to people is far more interesting and fun than talking about myself.*
19. *Joy is different than happiness. In all circumstances, joy can be found.*
20. *As the CEO of the Respond Well Department of my life, I am the only one responsible for how I react to things. No person or circumstances has the ability to cause me to respond poorly. I'm 100% responsible for that.*
21. *It's way more fulfilling and fun pursuing your dreams than it is trying to live up to someone else's expectations of you.*
22. *If you're reading this, you are stronger and more capable than you give yourself credit for. Do the hard things. Don't be afraid to fail. You will end up back on your feet. I promise.*

November 6th, 2021

This is a bank deposit of mine from 2003. (This post has a picture of a deposit slip of mine that had a positive 42 cents account balance)

Nicki and I were two years into our marriage. I was working full-time and she was at school more than full-time. We didn't have any savings and lived check to check. More times than not, there was more month than money, if you know what I mean.
This particular day we were negative $1.08 in our account. At 8 p.m. that night, we were going to get charged an overdraft fee of $36.
So, we tossed our house, looked in all the couch crevices, under the washer and dryer, in our cars, all over the place in order to find any loose change. We found $1.50 in various coins and I drove to the bank to make a deposit to bring us positive in our account to the tune of 42 cents. When the deposit slip printed out, I wrote, "Never forget how this feels. Consider it pure joy when you face trials of any kind." Then I wrote a sentence of gratitude underneath that, to remind myself of how fortunate that money problems were the only problems I was dealing with.
Now, 18 years later, I still have that deposit slip in my wallet to remind myself of one very important thing: that despite how hard things are or were, not to give up on yourself or your dreams. Whether you're a believer

or not, I can look back and see that God took care of all our needs and even some of our wants. "Logic" would have told me to reassess my life at that point and make a change that would have definitely given us more financial stability. But it would have been at the sacrifice of my dreams and desires.

Whether it's financial or not, if you're at a point in your life where you are experiencing difficulties in any area, don't give up on yourself. I'm walking proof that it WILL get better. And just to be clear, I'm not referring to finances specifically. I'm referring to the fact that the trials you're facing will not always be prominent in your life. Believe in yourself, trust God implicitly, and keep the hope that you'll achieve what you're going after.

October 20th, 2021

"A broken crayon can still do exactly what it was meant to do before it became broken."

Just because you are either literally broken or feeling broken inside, does not mean that you can't accomplish everything God has set out for you.

When I read the Bible, the theme I see over and OVER again is that God LOVES to make history with broken people.

If you're reading this, you are fully capable of "coloring" with your brokenness. Get up. Dust yourself off and get back into the battle.

July 29th, 2021

A long time ago in a galaxy far, far away, I was a waiter at the Olive Garden.
For over two years I had the time of my life there, during a really fun period in my early 20's. I also happened to meet Nicki there. But that's another story.

We had quite a few regulars who were known as good tippers. So when those people would walk in, all of the waiters would try to woo the hostesses to get those people sat in our section.
There were also people, quite frankly, that we knew were not good tippers, and we would try to avoid them getting sat in our section at all costs.
One particular Saturday, a family came in with five kids. Honestly, this family looked like they had no business going to eat at a restaurant, let alone a restaurant where they were going to drop the kind of money that seven people would be charged for at the OG.
As fate would have it, they were sat in my section. And I have to admit I remembered thinking to myself this

table was not going to be worth my time. (I know, how self-righteous of me.)

But I wasn't entirely a jerk at that age, so I did give them my best. I conversed with them, I spent time at their table, talked to their kids, and generally gave them really great service.

The bill ended up being right around $100, and I took it to the table. The father must've known how his family looked to everyone else, because he looked at me and said, "Thank you for treating us like we were human beings." He then pulled out two $100 bills and told me to keep the change. Then he shook my hand and said thanks again.

My point in telling this story is not to pat myself on the back. My lesson that day was a watershed moment in my life. I'd like to say from that day forward, I've never looked down on anyone just because of their appearance or what I might perceive to be "less than" compared to most.

The times we live in are times of great judgment. We have become so quick to judge others while at the same time forgetting that they too are made in the image and likeness of God, just like we are. I'm so thankful that family was sat in my section that day. Their generosity taught me a powerful lesson about how I think of myself compared to others. Beautiful things happen when you consider others as higher than yourself.

Truth be told, I had forgotten about a few of those posts. That's the great thing about journaling though! You might be going through something now that in five years will barely show up on your radar, but by journaling it you have gotten your feelings about it out. Rereading those entries was really cool because it reminded me once again that God's promises can be counted on. Some of those posts came at pretty dark times, but now, looking back, those were the times that grew me closer to God. They were part of the foundation that can never be shaken. If you want that solid foundation, however, that's a decision you're going to have to make. You're going to have to put your anchor far, far down in order for you not to be swayed back and forth when the waves hit.

If you don't currently journal, I highly recommend it. Not just for the ability to write through what you're experiencing in the moment, but years from now when your life is different, those entries will be honey to your soul. You'll realize that you were and are stronger than you give yourself credit for. Even if you legitimately suck at writing, it doesn't matter, because you're most likely the only one that will ever read your entries. And if you want to go the extra mile, put the pen to paper. I mentioned I forgot about a few of those Facebook posts, but I am looking at a journal on my desk that I took to Africa in 2009, and I remember every single entry in there. There's something special about pen and ink hitting paper.

CHAPTER 12

People That Inspire Me and Closing Thoughts

**Song for this Chapter:
Semisonic –** *Closing Time*

I forget who said it to me, but someone wiser (and probably older) than me once told me, "You always need to have a Paul and a Timothy in your life." The point being, you always need to have a mentor and someone you're mentoring. I've been fortunate to have three incredible mentors in my life. During my younger years, my 7th and 8th grade English teacher, Jaime Richards, took me under his wing for reasons beyond me. I was not the model student, I repeatedly disrupted his class, and on one occasion insulted him so disrespectfully that as he threw me out of class, he told me he hoped an upperclassman kicked my butt during lunch! Twenty-five years later, we are still in touch and even had lunch a few months ago. He's been a vocal supporter of my dreams the entire time I've known him, and he wrote me a beautiful "congratulations" card once I started filming The Talking Tree. As I got older and met my wife, Paul McGovern, the pastor of our church, took me under his wing, for unknown reasons. I'm seriously laughing out loud writing that because it's so true. Paul served as my spiritual guide during my early 20's and into my 30's. He was there to help me pick up the pieces when I was an idiot, and he too always supported me and encouraged me in following my dreams. We have also stayed in touch, and I even put him in *The Talking Tree* as an inmate! When I moved to Sacramento, I obviously couldn't maintain the same type of relationship with Paul, so the Lord saw fit that I find a new mentor and frankly, a spiritual father. Francis Anfuso, pastor (retired now) of the Rock of Roseville, and I hit it off from the moment we met. We both have the same passion for using media as a way to spread positive messages and God's Word, along with many other similarities that go beneath the surface. He's been in my life for over five years now, and I don't think this book would be a reality, nor me handling my mother's death in the way that I did, without him.

Those are three men in my life that I have met and have a relationship with. But there are two other men who I don't know (except for meeting them briefly) that also inspire me and encourage me through their videos, books, and social media posts. The first is someone I've mentioned a couple times in this book, and that is Mark Driscoll. Mark was a megachurch pastor seemingly at the height of popularity when his church in Washington state split, resulting in him leaving the church he started and moving to Arizona to start a new church. You want to talk about a guy who "responds well"? Well, look no further than him. Not only that, but his website, social media, and books are full of biblical teaching that is unapologetically honest and gritty, which is what this day and age needs. As I stated in the opening of this book, Mark's own book, Who Do You Think You Are" was a major catalyst for me fighting through a lot of my mind battles and low moments. I can't recommend his books and media enough. They are truly life-changing.

The other man is Bob Goff. Bob Goff is hilarious (like me, right?) and also extremely deep and full of wisdom. I happen to live within walking distance of the largest church in Northern California and have had the pleasure of hearing Bob speak in person a few times. In FACT, truth be told, he is the inspiration behind me giving my phone number and email address away in this book, because he puts his phone number in his books as well. And if Bob Goff does it, then certainly I can do it. Because if Bob Goff jumped off a bridge, so would I. Just kidding. I mean, unless it was one of those old-town bridges that's like three feet above the water. Anyway. Bob is a master at encouraging people to go after their dreams. The stories he tells, along with the experiences he's had, make him the real deal. I'm quite sure any one of Bob's books are infinitely better than this one, so at the very least, if you've been disappointed with this book, go read one of Bob's. It'll make up for it.

That's great, Ricky. What's the point of talking about those three guys? I'm glad you asked. In addition to my own biological father whom I love very much and my Heavenly Father whom I also love very much, the Lord knew I needed other "fatherly" men in my life who would help guide and encourage me along my path. I feel very fortunate and blessed to have the men in my life that I do. And I also realize that not every boy growing up has that same situation. That's why the second portion of what I was told is important. You need to have a Timothy in your life, someone younger (or older in some cases!) than you that you mentor/support/encourage. And I'm not talking about the type of relationship where once every six months you send a text. I'm talking about a relationship that's intentional and that you set aside time for. The most valuable gift you can give to someone is your time. And when you give that time to someone you're mentoring, it will absolutely make a world of difference.

A final thought on dreams and my favorite subject, ME. First, about your dreams. I just want to encourage you that no dream is too big. There are stories left and right about men and women who come from some of the worst parts of the world who achieved their dreams. There are stories of men and women who boldly flew in the face of "the norm," and achieved monumental success. There are stories of men and women coming from poverty that achieved incredible things in their lives. The point is, do not be afraid of the size of your dream. Don't talk yourself into settling for a dream that falls short of the best-case scenario. And don't talk yourself out of pushing through the hard times. Remember, if it were easy, everyone would be doing it.

Now, onto ME. I love me some ME. But in this case, I'm going to let you in on a secret about me: **I'm not special**. Meaning, God loves you and wants you to achieve your dreams just as much as he does me. The Bible says we are all God's favorites. Therefore, there's nothing in me that isn't in you. You're just as capable of achieving your dreams and having fun stories like the bridge toll story as I am. God wants you to have your own bridge toll story. I don't know when or how you'll have your bridge toll moment, but you will. God loves taking care of His kids. The last thing in the world He wants is for you to think that only certain people on earth were called to have and lead incredible lives. That life is in ALL of us if we'll trust Him and go after it. So do it. GO AFTER IT. It's going to be hard. It's going to be frustrating. You're going to lose friends. You'll disappoint family members. But as long as you keep your eyes on God and keep picking yourself up off the battlefield when you're knocked down, you WILL be able to *run with perseverance the race marked out for us*. You have it in you RIGHT NOW to start, endure and finish the race.

Will you take that first step?

Epilogue

As I sit here and think about the first day I began writing this book five-plus years ago and where my life is now, I can hardly believe it. I remember firing up my laptop and thinking I needed to start writing all this out because God would not let me stop thinking about it. It was an ugly, hand-me-down brown couch we had, inside of our three-bedroom rental. Now, two more kids later, I'm finishing this book while sitting at a desk in a different home we are renting, listening to EDM music while my wife cooks dinner and my five kids play throughout the house. In some ways, that day I began writing feels like five minutes ago, and in some ways, it feels like decades ago. The passing of my mother was the most significant difficult event, and the birth of two more children were the most significant awesome events. But through it all, the one thing that has remained unwavering has been God's love and promises in my life. He is literally the only reason I'm sitting here right now, putting the finishing touches on this book, and the beginning foundation on my career.

Mark Driscoll, a pastor and personal hero in the faith for me, says this phrase all the time: (Hey Mark, if you're reading this, I want to become BFF's. I know you live in Arizona and I'm in Tennessee, but we could Facetime and talk about football, raising a ton of kids, and sports. I'll be waiting for your call. DON'T LET ME DOWN!) "The most important thing about your life is what you think about Jesus Christ." If there was only one thing about this book you remember, I would hope it would be that. None of the other words in this book matter more than that phrase. What you think about Jesus is the most important thing about you. It's going to determine your earthly life, and it's going to determine your eternal life. So as you read the last few sentences of this book, I encourage you to take that sentence seriously. And for those of you reading this that aren't sure what you think about Jesus, I have a request. Don't let myself, your friends, your parents, or anyone or anything else paint the picture of who you think Jesus is. Go online, find a web version of the Bible, and read the book of Matthew so you can read Jesus' own words about who He was and what He was here on Earth to do. The red letters, as they call them, are the most important words in the history of the world. Take an hour to read them. I promise if nothing else, you won't regret it.

I hope this book has encouraged you, edified you, and given you hope for your present and future. Like I mentioned a few chapters back, feel free to email, text or call me. I'd love to hear your story and encourage you. I'd also love to hear what phrases and sentences you underlined and/or highlighted. Speaking of which, I want to reiterate something from earlier in the book, because it's so important to me. It's a sentence I had to tell myself over and over again when it came to allowing people to speak into my life. And that is: *those that have given up on their dreams are going to be the first ones to tell you to quit on yours.* I can't remember where I heard or saw that, but it's definitely something that stuck with me. Be careful who you let speak into your life. Trust me when I say it's far easier to remember and think about the negative comments than it is to think about the positive ones.

In closing, there are a lot of people I would like to thank for helping me get where I'm at. But inevitably, in trying to remember and thank everyone who has helped along the way, I will forget a few. So in an attempt to be gracious and sincere, I will say thank you to all of you who have been a part of my life in a positive way. Whether it was through a phone call, email, lunch together, comment on my social media or otherwise, I am grateful from the bottom of my heart for you. There were certain days that without your words and prayers, I would have packed it in. Thank you. I love you all.

God bless. And May the Force Be with You.

BONUS CHAPTER

Post-Pandemic, Incredible Hardships and Incredible Opportunities to Respond Well and Refocus Your Energy Toward Your Dreams

**Song for this Chapter:
Gene Wilder – *Pure Imagination***

In chapter 5, I talked a lot about "responding well." It's a lesson I've had to learn the hard way over the last few years. But thanks to my mentor and spiritual father, Francis Anfuso, it's made all the difference in the world for my life.

At the beginning of every year, people everywhere come up with their New Year's Resolutions, which is just a fancy way of saying "Hey, I want to do some things better in my life. So I'm going to commit to them because it's a new year." Well, as I write this chapter, we are just coming out of the pandemic, and I can't think of a more difficult and troubling stretch of time in my 45 years on earth. The last three years brought forth a lot of difficult and harrowing events for people worldwide. (There were also some incredible things that came out of it, too: revival in colleges, people focusing more on family and interpersonal relationships once things opened back up, innovations in technology, working from home becoming more mainstream, just to name a few!)

But as I said, there were also a lot of not positive things that happened during the pandemic. (Feel free to research that yourself, as I'm certainly not going to remind anyone!)

The forced "stay at home" order during that time was extremely difficult for everyone. Lost lives, lost jobs, lost revenue, increased anxiety, increased fear, increased anger. People on all sides of the discussion are pointing fingers at each other. Blame was and is being thrown around by everyone. In some ways it's still truly an ugly and difficult time.

As the father of five children, the days have been long, and the frustration my children have had in not being able to go outside, not being able to see their friends, not being able to graduate properly, etc., has been hard for not only them, but my wife as well. I can only imagine that everyone was feeling that kind of frustration and anxiety to a degree. I hate to admit it, but I even had my moments of being down during all of it. I hate admitting that because I try my best to remain positive no matter what. But we are all human and we all have our breaking points. I've found mine a couple times. The key for me being able to move past those feelings was something I mentioned earlier in the book, which is having people in my life who love and support me, whom I can call or text when I'm feeling down and empty. I can't stress enough how important it is for you to not run your race by yourself. It's imperative you allow people in your life who can encourage you.

Okay, enough about that aspect of the pandemic.

I want to focus on another aspect, which is something I realized a few weeks ago after contemplating the contents of this book: I believe this pandemic has the ability to provide you an incredible opportunity to take stock of your life, your career, your dreams and your future, and make adjustments if necessary. When we were all forced to stay home, a lot of people quickly realized that their position at their company was "nonessential." And a lot of those people were let go or laid off. Some businesses as a whole didn't make it. It became clear in a matter of weeks that what we all thought was "secure" and "taken care of" most certainly was not. Pensions, retirement funds, 401k accounts and the like were all decimated. What seemed unshakable was shaken.

But you know what else I saw come out of those difficulties related to the pandemic? I saw a lot of people start talking about what they were going to do once the shelter in place orders were lifted. "I'm going to go there." "I'm going to do this." "I'm going to spend more time doing this and that…" Being forced to stay at home re-racked people's minds to think about what was and is truly important in life: relationships and experiences.

And for me, the hope I have right now for all my friends and family, who are at home spending a lot more time thinking about what's important, is the same hope I have for you right now: When things go "back to normal", I want you to be zealous for pursuing your dreams. If you've lost your job, your 401k, your desire to work in a field that you're not interested in, then **now is the perfect time** to pursue your dreams and bet on yourself. (You're not really "betting," by the way. God wants you to succeed. But "bet on yourself" is a cool phrase and I wanted to use it.) If you're at what you consider a low point, if things are hard and you don't know what to do when we're given the all-clear, then why not make your dreams a priority? Why NOT open that hot dog stand?

I realize that by the time you're reading this, the COVID pandemic should be in our rear-view mirrors. But here's the thing, you don't need a pandemic to usher change into your life. Life is already full of "pandemics." But if you decide to respond well to them, you're not only multiple steps ahead of the game, but you can turn those "pandemics" into opportunities to have something wonderful come from them.

They say the only place you can go when you're down is up. Well, why not make your new "up" something that excites you in the core of your being? Since a lot of us are starting at square one again right now, imagine what the "new normal" could look like if everyone began pursuing their dreams and living happier, more fulfilling lives?

"If you want to view paradise
Simply look around and view it
Anything you want to, do it
Want to change the world?
There's nothing to it."

Wise words from Willy Wonka. So press that red button in the Wonkavator that Charlie pressed. Take it to the top floor and then **break through** the ceiling of your life. There's no better view, and there's no better feeling.

Printed in the USA
CPSIA information can be obtained
at www.ICGtesting.com
LVHW080917010324
773138LV00013B/501